CECILIA ESTHER

WESTBOW
PRESS®
A DIVISION OF THOMAS NELSON
& ZONDERVAN

WestBow Press books may be ordered through booksellers or by contacting:

WestBow Press
A Division of Thomas Nelson & Zondervan
1663 Liberty Drive
Bloomington, IN 47403
www.westbowpress.com
844-714-3454

ISBN: 978-1-6642-1130-8 (sc)
ISBN: 978-1-6642-1131-5 (hc)
ISBN: 978-1-6642-1129-2 (e)

Library of Congress Control Number: 2020921653

Print information available on the last page.

WestBow Press rev. date: 3/26/2021

Contents

Introduction: How Did I Get Here?.................................... vii

PART ONE

1   Before the Fall 1
2   A Punch in the Gut 6
3   Putting on the Armor of God............................. 11
4   Footprints in the Sand...................................... 16
5   Livin' the Dreams.. 21
6   The Battle Begins 28
7   A Billboard Sign 35
8   Thy Will Be Done... 39
9   A Flash of Emotion.. 44
10 The First Miracle.. 48
11 Forged by Fire 54
12 The Man from Missouri..................................... 60
13 The Truth Hurts... 66

PART TWO

14 God Makes Me Slow Down 75
15 Anger Wrapped Up in Prayer............................. 81
16 Tears That Heal.. 88
17 Show Some Faith 97
18 Everything Happens for a Reason 103

PART THREE

19 Another Miracle 115

20 How Could You? 123

21 The Answer is NO 129

22 Endings and Beginnings... 135

23 The Key and the Crown 141

24 Love What Loves You Back.. 150

Introduction: How Did I Get Here?

It is not easy to write these words. I have a story to tell, but it is filled with pain and tears. It is also filled with great joy and happiness, but I am struggling to know where or how to begin. There is a lot of backstory that I could fill in with details and many emotions that I want to share but that would take a lot of time and a lot of emotion. I guess I will follow in the fashion of all storytellers, and begin at the beginning...

In the Winter of 2005, I married the love of my life. This man showed me kindness, love, and great friendship. He often told me how he fell in love with me over the telephone, when we were just beginning to be friends. I knew I loved him the moment I witnessed his great love for his mother: How he gazed at her, eyes full of love and compassion, opening the car door for her, dancing with her at the Eagles Club, and always being willing to lend his helping hands to her needs. We knew we were going to marry each other at the end of our first vacation together, nine months into dating.

Even my grandmother loved him. He was such the gentleman and quite a looker too, as she would put it. My grandma said with his dark hair, intense green eyes, and 6-foot-three-inch tall frame coupled with my blue eyes and blond hair and natural beauty we would make beautiful babies someday. I remember that had made me so excited with thoughts for our future family. It seemed I had met the man of my dreams; I had even told him that one night when he had asked me what kind of guy was my type? We had laughed together when he stepped back, reintroduced himself to me and said, 'here I am, the man of your dreams, at your service!'

Let me back up. The night we first met; I was at a party organized by an old high school boyfriend. I was there with hopes of rekindling some of those sparks with Wyatt; we had been talking on the phone and hanging out together, inconsistently, for a few weeks. It felt much like a cat-and-mouse game and I was, in truth, growing tired of it. That night at the party there was a young man there that I had never met before. He was tall, dark-haired, and had these intensely green eyes that seemed to look straight into my heart. I could not seem to take my eyes off him the entire night even though there was another young woman there that was obviously connected to him somehow.

At one point in the evening, I remember him coming over to sit next to me on the couch and striking up a conversation with me. He told me his name was Cody and that he had been watching me all night. I laughed and admitted to him that I had been trying to be inconspicuous as I was staring at him all night too. Not only was there an exchange of body heat as we sat so closely next to each other, secretly exchanging our truths to each other, but there was a magnetic pull of attraction between us that I could tell we were both feeling in these moments.

I asked him about the woman that had been stuck to his side so closely until now. Who was she? Where did she suddenly go? He confessed to me that she was, in fact, his girlfriend and she left the party with one of her "guy" friends. Hearing the word "girlfriend," I created physical space between us and started doubting my initial feelings. He closed that space, moved closer to me again, and attempted to explain how they were not as happy as it may have appeared while they were dancing. I listened while he explained, but I was skeptical.

That skepticism eventually wore away over time as the days turned into weeks and Cody called me every evening. We began a friendship over the phone and talked about everything under the sun. One night during our conversation, he told me he was planning to end his relationship with his girlfriend. When I asked him why, he explained that it was not going where he thought he'd wanted it to go before, his feelings had changed, and he wanted out. I listened to him but made it clear that I did not want to be the reason that he was breaking up with someone. While I liked him, I was also happy being the really good friends that we had become.

Our friendship stayed platonic like that for months. He did break it off with his girlfriend at that time, but he and I did not become romantically involved right away. It was not until nearly 5 months later that I finally mustered up enough courage to invite him to be my date for a wedding. Having the relationship we did, he did not hesitate to agree to escort me to the wedding. During the two-hour drive North to the lake destination, I do not remember pausing once in our conversation. We held hands at the wedding ceremony and when the newly married couple visited our table during the reception, my two long-time friends that had married each other that day looked at me with a sideways glance, then at different times that night asked me, "So, you really like this guy, huh?"

That night was our first date. Actually, that weekend was our first, second, and third dates. It all started from there and just continued to get better and better.

We had a way of being able to balance each other. When I was angry, he was calm. When he was spitting nails, I could talk him down and we would weather the storm together. I looked forward to coming home from work to see him so I could tell him about my day, and he would share events that he went through with me. It was an easy love and lifestyle that made me incredibly happy. We had fun together and were each other's best friend. Our life together was blessed with this loving give and take sort of existence. From the very beginning we knew there was no such thing as divorce in our vocabulary, let alone our lives.

For almost nine years that was true. In the Summer of 2012, everything changed. A series of events occurred that caused my world to come crashing down around me. The man I knew and loved suddenly became another person. Regardless of what I said or did to try to influence him and save our marriage he was unreachable. I did not know how to deal with the hurt, anguish, and frustration that enveloped me.

Looking back, this story is not so much about the events that occurred that destroyed my marriage and life as I knew it. This story is about the way that Jesus carried me through this nightmare; how God made the silver lining in this storm cloud blaze bright; and how the Holy Spirit spoke to me. This story is about the proof that miracles can and do still happen today.

PART

ONE

1

Before the Fall

We had tried for years to have a baby. Infertility tests, bloodwork, insemination, endometriosis surgeries, months of charting through natural family planning, hormone injections, and painful miscarriages all resulted in one thing: no baby. Except this time was going to be different. In the Spring of 2012, a young girl approached us, wanting us to adopt her unborn baby. Hesitant and scared, we talked at length about the pros and cons of the situation.

"I need to talk to your dad," my husband said. "He's had five kids. He'll tell me honestly what to do."

I told him "Okay, let's go." Even though it was ten o'clock at night by this time. I was glad to hear that he wanted to reach out to my parents for guidance. This was definitely a situation where we should be seeking guidance from any source that would be willing to talk all aspects of it out with us. The baby was supposed to be due in July and we had little time to decide. I had prayed for so long that we would have a family together, I was certain this was our time.

Once we wrapped our heads around this idea and my husband was able to start planning the logistics of the situation out, he told me he was going to trust my faith on this. He told me he believed that even though there was a great risk involved in this potential adoption case, he didn't think that I would choose to go through with it unless I truly believed it was in our best interest. I told him that I was also nervous about it but that I really believed we could make it work and that we would be happy.

Over the next few weeks, we planned, shopped for the nursery, and told our extended families about our plans. I even attended several doctor appointments with the birthmother and witnessed the final ultrasound before delivery. We were so excited and thankful to have this opportunity land in our laps after seven and a half years of marriage. Over the three to four weeks of preparation, I remember just praying to God that the baby and the mother would be healthy and thanking him for this opportunity.

Around eleven o'clock p.m. on July 1 the birth mom texted me, saying she thought she was having labor pains. She told me not to worry and that she would let me know when or if she went to the hospital as they could be Braxton Hicks. I did not wake my husband; he had to be up early to work the next morning and I wanted him to rest if he could until I knew for sure what was happening. Somewhere around four in the morning the birth mom texted me again, saying she was at the hospital and they were getting ready to put her in a room. She told me not to run to the hospital yet; she planned to text me as soon as the doctor or nurse told her how long it would be until she delivered. She said she did not want us to have to sit out and wait around too long. I must admit a warning bell went off in my mind- *but I thought what do I know? It must be hard going into delivery knowing you're going to give up your baby to another woman.* I told myself to give her some space. My husband had already left for work, so I didn't think it could hurt to wait.

By six in the morning I had received another text message telling me how sorry she was and that she just could not go through with the adoption. She told me the birthfather had come to the hospital and he was going to be there for her, and that they were going to raise the baby together. She ended by saying again how sorry she was and begging me to please understand. I remember sitting in the bathroom alone in the dawning of the day with tears streaming down my face, knowing that here we were again: empty-handed with no baby and a full nursery.

Worse yet, my husband had no idea. So, what did I do? I picked myself up off the floor, took a shower, and went into work. I decided that no action was the best action for the moment. I would deal with it later. When we were both home from work later that afternoon, we would be able to sit down together and process it as a couple. We could handle it together.

At one o'clock that afternoon I was driving home from work when my husband called me on my cell phone. He asked me if I'd heard from the birth mom. I could not lie to him and it all came tumbling out of my mouth before I could stop it. There was complete silence on the other end of the phone line.

I spoke his name.

He said, "Okay. I'm going to have to deal with that later. I'm on my way down to Memorial Hospital. They are life-flighting my dad right now and my mom's in the truck with me. You should go home and rest."

My breath caught in my throat and said, "No, I'm fine. I'm turning the car around. I'll meet you at the hospital." I hung up the phone, stunned. Almost immediately, I did a U-turn in the nearby grocery store parking lot and simultaneously called my sister for help. She worked for Physicians Medical, a subsidiary of Memorial Hospital; she would know what to do and who to contact.

Pulling into the hospital parking garage and repeating the Lord's Prayer and the Hail Mary prayer all the way, we arrived to discover my father-in-law was being scheduled for immediate heart surgery. He had been diagnosed with having a heart attack, caused by blocked arteries, namely the one they call the widow-maker for its high mortality rate. My mother-in-law almost immediately pulled me into the hallway and enveloped me into a huge hug. She whispered through choked back tears how sorry she was to hear about the baby and the lost adoption. Tears threatened to surface, but I shrugged them away and explained to her that it was okay. I could not mourn what I never had. The fact that I was with my family at that moment and my father-in-law mattered most. I told her that the family I already had meant more to me than any potential family.

"We just need to pray that your husband will make it through this surgery and recover" I told her, giving her the tightest hug, I thought she could handle in the moment. And I meant every word. Suddenly it was like the fog had lifted and what meant the most to me was realized. My existing family was so important. I prayed to God that my father-in-law would be okay.

Thank God, he was! He came out of that surgery and grew stronger and more determined to live a healthy lifestyle and has stayed committed to that to this day. Something however, snapped in my husband. My mother-in-law tells the story of watching him slowly walk to the life flight helicopter with a firm jaw set, shoulders back, chest out, and a white-knuckle grip on her husband's hand as if he was carrying the weight and stress of everyone involved that day. It was as if by his very mindset he could stave off anything bad from happening to his dad.

Every day after that for a week my husband held onto that tight grip of control he had on his emotions. He looked at me and others as if daring us to ask what was wrong just so he could explode. He would soften for moments to ask me if I was okay about the adoption. I answered him the same way I answered everyone, and I meant it: I was okay. I never had anything this time, so I never lost anything. He also took it upon himself to return (without me) every item we'd purchased for the nursery to the store.

Two weeks later, my husband had a hard time getting up off the couch. He would go to work and come home and spend the rest of the day watching TV or sleeping. I would ask him if he wanted to do something, or we would get an invitation from friends, but he'd say no. I asked him what was wrong and one time he told me, "It's not you: it's me. I've just got to sort this out in my head, and I'll be okay. I promise." I had no idea what that could possibly mean but I accepted it and tried to support him through it. He sometimes had moments of "blue" behavior before and we had laughed about it, calling it seasonal depressive disorder or the winter blues.

I thought I understood where his emotions were coming from. His dad had a heart attack on the same day we lost an adoption and he was helpless to control either situation. I felt like he had every right to go through a little depression. Even though he had been with me through all the other infertility trials, miscarriages, and surgeries, he had never had to experience the loss firsthand in the same way that I did. I just thought this time it had hit home much harder, especially with his dad's sickness on top of everything.

2

A Punch in the Gut

By August things had seemingly started to improve. My birthday was coming on the eighteenth and he told me he was sure he would be 100 percent better by then. I was still worried that he needed medicine, but I was glad to hear that he thought there was an end in sight, and he had started acting more like his old self. We had heard from the lawyer that some of the money we'd invested in the adoption would be refunded to us. Just the other day we took the boat out to the lake and had one of the best days ever! We went swimming in a cove, cuddled together like a couple in love, and he even laughed about the silly things we were daring each other to do while hidden behind the privacy of the boat. It felt like one of our early married days again.

On the day after my birthday, around five in the afternoon, my husband came home in a bad mood after being with his father and brother at a golf outing. I asked him why? I thought he should be in a good mood from golfing all day.

He answered me saying, "I'm not happy."

I said, "I know. That's why I asked you what's wrong?"

He looked at me and said, "I'm not happy in our marriage."

All the air rushed out of my lungs in that moment. What he said made no sense. I couldn't even process any thoughts except that it felt like I'd been punched in the gut. Unable to breathe, I stumbled out of our bedroom towards the garage and into my car. I had to get out of the house. I had to go somewhere and process what seemed like the ugliest possible statement I could have heard and the fact that I had just been sideswiped with it.

I drove around in the countryside, parked in the neighborhood green space, then finally came back home thirty or forty minutes later. I pulled the car back into the driveway to find my husband outside on his cellphone. He quickly hung up and watched me step out of the car. When I did, he asked, "Would you like to talk about this now?"

"Would YOU like to talk about this now?" I asked him back. I felt like it was his job to explain himself, as I had no clue from where any of this had come.

Over the next few weeks there were more tears than answers. He kept insisting there was no other woman, no real reason for him wanting space. He just kept saying that he was not happy and needed to clear his mind. I remember waking up one morning and going out to the kitchen to find him getting ready for work. For some reason, the thought of divorce entered my mind. I told him we were not getting a divorce, even though he hadn't actually said those words to me yet. He told me again he just was not happy.

I exploded, nearly screaming at him, "Well then, you better fake it 'til you make it because we agreed a long time ago there wasn't any such thing as divorce!"

It was then that this angry look swept over his face, like how dare I challenge him? That made me even angrier. I had been tiptoeing around my own house for weeks trying to figure out what had happened to our love story and here he was ready to just throw in the towel without even trying to fix things. He had already told me he would not go to counseling with me. He had stopped going to church with me as well, opting instead to work the weekends. I was at a loss. Marriages had rough spots, couples were supposed to talk and work through them together. How were we going to get through this when he would not even talk to me? That was how we fell in love, by talking to each other!

Labor Day weekend arrived in a cloud of tense silence. One night of that weekend we managed to be sitting out on the back deck, drinking a beer together. I asked him to please tell me what his reasons were for being so unhappy with me. After a long pause, he looked at me, took a draw from his beer, and said, "I think we're on our way out."

For the second time in less than two months, I physically felt the air swoosh from my lungs. I asked him why? I mentioned marriages have stumbling blocks, that we had made it through so many years and through some stressful things together. "How could we be on our way out?"

He said, "We don't have anything left to talk about. I am done with the baby talk. There's nothing left."

Tears filled my eyes. Did he honestly think that was the only thing I was concerned with? Yes, maybe, that had consumed me, but I loved him! He was my world! I tried to convey these thoughts to him immediately. I reminded him of vacations we have taken together, our times out on the lake in our boat, the fun we've had with family and friends, and how we'd built this life together—all without children. I even quoted from him a long time ago when he told me we would be our own family if we were unable to conceive.

His gaze was locked away from me. He was not listening to me. My words were not getting through to him. His facial features were contorted and set into an unrecognizable visage. Who was this man sitting across the table from me? What happened to my husband?

Another day, I remember coming home from work around 6 p.m., having worked a little later than usual, pulling into the driveway, and seeing my husband sitting outside on the front porch. This was our usual meeting spot after work when we just wanted to chill before ending the day officially inside the house. It looked so much like the days of old, I felt my shoulders relax a little. I parked the car and approached him, cautiously smiling at him, and said hello. He handed me a beer and asked how was my day? We chatted about inconsequential small talk items for a few moments and I could feel myself relaxing even a bit more with the passing minutes. He told me in a little while he was going up to the bar to meet his brother for a drink and play some pool.

"Before I go into town to meet my brother, I want to show you some things," he told me while standing up from the porch, indicating that I should follow him.

We walked into the garage and he started to fiddle with the red snowblower in the southwest corner. He maneuvered it out into the open space and started explaining how the snobs and cranks and pulleys worked to start up and make the machine blow the snow off the driveway. "Why are you telling me this?" I questioned him. He answered plainly, matter-of-factly, "Because when I leave, you're going to have to know how to operate all these different kinds of equipment by yourself."

My head started to spin, literally, the insides of my brain were swirling in every direction with that feeling of the world tipping upside down. I would see that my vision was starting to blur and distort, and I ran out of the garage, back towards the front porch. I did not make it to the chairs though, collapsing in the grass and falling to my knees. I started vomiting violently, straight streams of liquid amber mixed with bile.

My husband approached me, sounding confused, perplexed even, but oddly distant. "What's wrong? Why are you getting sick?" He asked. "Are you okay?" He asked that last question still from a distance. Shouldn't he be offering me a towel, or a tissue? Or pulling my hair back from my face like before?

I looked up at him, from my place on the ground, where I had just puked and almost passed out from pure emotions, panic, and heartsickness. How could I explain that feeling of trauma to a person that was standing there still as a statue, looking at me like he had no idea why I was even a little upset. Like he was simply explaining a normal procedure of how to start a snowblower because he was going away on a business trip. What was wrong with him?

I stood up, shakily, and wiped my mouth with the back of my hand. "I guess I wasn't expecting that" was all I could think of to tell him. He looked at me a while longer then said, "Well, I'm gonna go head out and meet my brother now."

Sometime shortly after that, the days all blur together now, my husband told me he would be moving out by the end of October. This seemed so absurd to me. If things were so bad in our marriage that he had to move out, so bad that he couldn't even bare to go to a counselor to even *attempt* to save our future together, how could he stand to live in the same house with me for the next thirty days?

This was torturing me! To come home at the end of each day, needing to unwind and relax from a stressful job but knowing that when I opened the door, I was only walking into the most important aspect of my life unraveling in front of my very eyes. Daily, this was absolutely ripping me apart from the inside out. I was holding myself together all day long at work, managing and leading an urban elementary school where I had told no one of my home-life struggles. How could I? It was the duty of the school principal to keep everything together; how could they trust me to run the over 640 enrolled students and more than 55 teachers and support staff if I could not keep one marriage together?

Something snapped in my mind, just a tiny bit. I felt a fire in my chest, and I remembered my dad telling me back in August that I should throw all his stuff out on the front lawn back on that very first day and change the locks. I knew at this moment I should have done just that.

If my husband was telling me he was going to move out, he was never coming back. This make-believe story of him needing time to sort things out and it may be a while before he can get back to his old self was just that—a tall tale he was feeding me. I told him NO. He looked at me quizzically.

I said again stronger this time, "No. If things are so bad here that you **have** to move out, you need to move out now. There is no need to wait thirty days. You can go stay with your brother or your mom and dad, but you don't need to live here!" With those words and that tiny spark of strength out of my body, I walked out of the door and got in my car leaving him to think about what I had just said for once.

3

❧᪐᪐᪐᪐

Putting on the Armor of God

With tears streaming down my face and betraying my true emotions, I drove to see friends that night. They commiserated with me and told me they thought it was the right thing to do. They thought surely, he would come to his senses more quickly if he had to struggle on his own and be alone with his thoughts to realize how we were meant to be together. His own brother told me to "Hold on as long as you possibly can. It might take him a long time, but I think he'll come to his senses." Those were words I desperately needed and wanted to hear. Oh, how I longed for them to be true...

Never one to have the power of irony lost on me, I realized at church one Sunday morning that Pope Benedict had decreed 2012 the Year of Marriage. I thought to myself maybe that was the answer: I needed to pray more. Satan was attacking my marriage; my husband had just been baptized in the Catholic Church at Easter Vigil Mass in 2011. This fight was not between me and my husband per se, it was between us and evil.

That night, while my husband slept on the air mattress in the guest bedroom, I took the bottle of holy water and sprinkled it over him while praying the Lord's Prayer. He bolted upright in bed, out of a dead sleep, his face contorted exclaiming, "What are you soaking me with?!" I drew back, not expecting such a venomous reaction from a few drops of holy water. I told him what it was, and he yelled at me to leave him alone, asking me if I was crazy? Whoa, I thought to myself. I think I may have stumbled onto something here. I needed to start praying. I needed to get ready to do battle! I turned to the Bible and found these words, not by chance I believe. "He armed himself with weapons of war…for victory in war does not depend on the size of the army, but on the strength that comes from Heaven" (1 Maccabees 3:3, 19-20).

The next evening after work we were sitting out on the front porch talking about our respective days at work. It felt a little different today, but still had that uncomfortable edge to it. He asked if he could ask me a question.

I said, "Of course, I'm your wife."

He said, "You might not want to help me with this question." He began to explain that he had started to look at places to live. I started holding my breath, thinking *"I can never get peace… He's got a lot of nerve…"*

He continued, "I really don't have anyone else to talk about this with. You have always been the one that's helped me sort out my thoughts. I would really appreciate it if you would help me consider these options."

As convoluted as this was, it was the truth. I let him continue, I felt like maybe he was trying to reach for something and if I just let him talk it out, he would realize how bad an idea it all was. He was trying to decide between an apartment and an old farmhouse, which was cheaper to rent because he would have to work on repairing it in exchange for the rent each month. The details rolled out over the course of the next thirty or so minutes and if one wasn't aware of all the back story of this situation and just took a snapshot of our conversation, one would think things were normal here.

Amidst this conversation tiny pinholes were poking into my heart, but I tried not to let him see that. Each word he uttered stabbed at me internally and I consciously withheld a flinch. At the end I told him my opinion, which was that he had a lot on his mind and if he started renovating a farmhouse he would concentrate only on that instead of the other things and he would never leave that farmhouse until it was finished. He could change his mind in an apartment and get out of the lease whenever he chose.

After a pause in which he looked like he was considering my input, I told him I was hoping that he would be able to sort these things out in his mind and come home. I told him that the door was open for him, no matter how long it might take him to come home to me. At that moment he caught my eyes, took my hand in his, and said to me, "Do you know how long it might take for me to feel like my old self again?"

To the outsider those words might have been cause for a stumble or a loss of faith. Instead they gave me hope. I felt like he was telling me there was a chance; that what his brother had told me was true, that there was no other woman or no other reason for this to be happening. I just needed to hold on long enough for my husband to come back to his senses and come back to the life and the wife everyone knew he loved. We had both cried real tears at our wedding: Tears of love, tears of happiness. So much so that each wedding we attended after our own we would look at each other, then compare it to ours and ask if we felt that "magic" that we felt during our marriage vows. I just really believed I needed to have faith here.

October seventh seemed like it was world marriage appreciation day at church. The readings were about marriage and how Jesus hates divorce. At least that is how I remember hearing it. I also remember thinking that it was a sign that my thoughts were right; I had to have faith. It was the Year of Marriage according to the Pope; my marriage was under siege from some unknown force; today's readings were meant to inspire me. If Jesus hates divorce and I certainly did not want to get divorced; we were on the same side of this fight! If Jesus was FOR me, then who could be against me? Surely, I was going to win this battle.

The very next day, on October 8, my husband moved out.

My heart was shattered into a million pieces! First, the stabbing pain invaded and the shortness of breath. Rather quickly, the tears flooded my eyes and rolled down my face in huge crashing waves. I stumbled through the house looking at items he left behind and the life we had spent ten years together building. Everywhere I looked seemed fractured and incomplete without him beside me, holding me up as my mind began to spin in a thousand different directions.

I found myself in the middle of the living room floor, crumpled into a heap, rubbing my hand up and down the frieze carpet, eyes turned upwards toward the lithograph photo I had bought him as a rehearsal dinner present nearly eight years ago. The poem spoke about a couple holding hands and making it through life until their golden years together. I had chosen him! We had done everything right: We waited to live together before marriage, we tried to have a family, he became Catholic, our families got along, I thought we had the perfect life… What happened to us?

I do not know how long I stayed on the floor that first night, but I eventually picked myself up and climbed into bed. Many more evenings after work repeated this same pattern. Make it through the workday, rush home to the safety of my house where I didn't have to pretend to keep it all together. I could fall apart in the privacy and security of my house where I was alone--- alone, alone, alone.

I prayed. I cried. I read the Bible. I cried again. Somewhere in the fog I began to watch EWTN. I cried some more. Mother Angelica's sweet voice had a way of soothing me and comforting me into thinking that even though it felt like my whole world was falling apart and I had no idea how to pick up the pieces and move on that I could do it anyway. She would remind me that Jesus said, "Let not your heart be troubled. That means you can do something about it." I started to pray the Rosary with Mother Angelica nightly. I set the DVR for the Chaplet of Saint Michael the Archangel and some nights I would fall asleep to the cherubic sound of the choir singing while I gripped the Rosary beads tightly in my hands.

The dreams started coming sometime in December. Huge, epic battles where I was amid a battlefield, drenched in blood, fallen horses and soldiers all around, a giant sword in my hands. I would wake in the middle of the night, scared, and confused. Why was I dreaming of this kind of battle?

One of my friends took the time to explain it to me. She told me that I was still under spiritual attack. Just because my husband had left, it did not mean that the battle was over! She started quoting scripture.

She read to me, "Do not fear or be dismayed because of this great multitude, for the battle is not yours but God's" (2 Chronicles 20:15). She explained that I am in a war with an enemy that I needed God to help me fight. She told me the best weapon I had was prayer. She said I had to trust that God's plan was better than my plan; she said she knew that I was anxious and worried but she quoted, "For God gave us a spirit not of fear but of power and love and self-control" (2 Timothy 1:7).

When I turned to my Bible this night, I found more words of strength. Remembering that I did not go looking for these words but instead stumbled across them ignited in me a strong belief that God was speaking to me and trying to firm up my conviction that I could get through this trying time as long as I stayed close to him.

"Finally, my brethren, be strong in the Lord and in the power of His might. Put on the whole armor of God, that you may be able to stand against the wiles of the devil. For we do not wrestle against flesh and blood, but against principalities, against powers, against rulers of the darkness of this age, against hosts of wickedness in the heavenly places. Therefore, take up the whole armor of God, that you may be able to withstand in the evil day, and having done all, to stand. Stand therefore, having girded your waist with truth, having put on the breastplate of righteousness, and having shod your feet with the preparation of the gospel of peace; above all, taking the shield of faith with which you will be able to quench all the fiery darts of the wicked one. And take the helmet of salvation, and the sword of the spirit, which is the word of God; praying always with all prayer and supplication in the Spirit, being watchful to this end with all perseverance and supplication for all the holy ones and also for me, that speech may be given me to open my mouth, to make known with boldness the mystery of the gospel for which I am an ambassador in chains, so that I may have the courage to speak as I must" (Ephesians 6:10-20).

4

Footprints in the Sand

On our eighth wedding anniversary, I had begun praying for the miracle. Well, truth be told I had prayed for several miracles. I knew God was with me and that the Holy Spirit was in the middle of inspiring me. The person I didn't feel that I knew well enough was Jesus. I remember kneeling at my bed this night my body just racking with sobs and praying to God to let me know his Son. I prayed to Mary to ask her Son to help me. I had married the love of my life, but he had left me for reasons that I had no clue. I was distraught to the point my dogs had given up trying to console me. I begged through sobs and hiccups, "Jesus, carry me! Please, I cannot do this on my own anymore. I need your help!"

In my mind's eye I saw Jesus in the Garden of Gethsemane, his hands folded on the rock ledge asking his Father to let his cup pass him by; much like I had been praying that God would grant me the miracle of fixing my marriage and sending my husband back to me. At the same time, I felt a peace come over me and a feeling that I was being comforted and that I was okay. Nothing had changed except the tears had stopped flowing and the hiccups were gone. I was still slumped over my bed and no husband had come waltzing through the door but there was a definite feeling of cool relief washing over me. It was as if a gentle hand was placed consolingly on my shoulder and the words, "Daughter, I am here. You are fine." were whispered softly into my ear. The heavy weight and sense of doom was gone from my shoulders. When I lifted my head from the bed, my vision was clear. In that moment I realized things were changing.

My friend bought me a journal and encouraged me to write down everything that was happening. She told me it might be important to remember dates and events. I decided to take it a step further and use the journal to not only chronicle my thoughts but to also match them up with my daily conversations with God and my Bible readings. The readings and the thoughts that form this story are matched up not by choice but by how they happened in real life. I would open my journal, write down my thoughts, feelings, and events of the day then open the Bible to a random selection and read. Before I would read, I would often ask God for help in discerning what he might want me to know about my situation or what thoughts he would like to point out to me. The results I found, to me, were miraculous and a true testament that HE was with me during this whole tumultuous time: guiding me, inspiring me, and keeping me faithful. Without Jesus carrying me, and the Word of God inspiring me, and God's strength supporting me, I never would have been able to even start this battle, much less make it through this long journey, at which point we've only just begun…

January thirteenth was the Feast of the Holy Family. It was also the ninth and final day of my novena to the Holy Family and my novena to Saint Michael the Archangel. I was barely watching any television these days; I was in full-on prayer mode. I had even made it to my first ever Eucharistic Adoration. Let me tell you, that was something awesome! I had no idea it would be so interesting, and freeing, and close with the Lord all at the same time.

Anyway, January thirteenth was the Feast Day of the Holy Family… For some reason, the thought came into my mind that what if all the dates of the past few months were aligned on purpose and not coincidental? I mean, I genuinely believe everything happens for a reason. In Jeremiah 29:11 it says, "For I know the plans I have for you says the Lord. Plans for good and not for evil, to give you a future and a hope."

At this point, my husband had been gone for three long months. Despite this agony I was able to realize there have been many, many blessings that have occurred because of this marriage separation:

1. I have lost 60 pounds since July.
2. I have had so much time with my mom and dad.
3. I have realized how much I love my mother-in-law and father-in-law.
4. I have realized how much I love and how much my brothers and sisters love me and how much we support each other.
5. I have realized that having a baby is not as important to me as being with and spending time loving and enjoying my existing family.
6. I have realized I didn't put God first in my life or in our marriage.
7. I have realized that I didn't listen to my husband's needs or how much I took him for granted.
8. I have realized my friends love and support me more than I gave them credit for.
9. I have realized how much I do love God, Jesus, Holy Spirit, Mary, Joseph, the Saints, and the Church.
10. Many people have been praying.
11. Ultimately, I have grown closer to God.

Even though I am so grateful for all these wonderful events and realizations of true feelings, I am suddenly overtaken by an overwhelming sense of loss. At 7:52 p.m. on January 13… In tears, I ask God for a sign that my husband will come back to me. Again, I pray for the miracle—as I have begun calling it. In almost the same breath, I feel terribly guilty and I apologize to God for not being patient and for struggling to trust Him. I also apologize for being selfish in my desires. There are so many bigger, more important problems in the world, and I know this!

He shows me Isaiah 21: 1-17. "I will put an end to all groaning… Go station a watchman, let him tell what he sees… Fallen, fallen is Babylon, and all the images of her gods are smashed to the ground... Watchman, how much longer the night?... Morning has come and again the night. If you will ask, ask; come back again... For thus says the Lord to me: In another year, like those of a hireling all the glory of Kedar shall come to an end." I wonder to myself if this means this will all be over in a year? It is January 2013. By 2014 will my husband be back? To me at the time I remember thinking Babylon was bad, my husband falling for another woman was bad. The reading said groaning would be over and Babylon would fall. That had to be good news for me, right? Could I legitimately interpret it that way?

The very next night ends again in tears for me. Tonight, I can't stop crying. It has been two weeks since I cried like this! It has also been two weeks since I talked to my husband. When will this torture end? I cannot seem to let him go. I never thought our marriage would ever come to this. How can I love someone so much who does not love me? Even though my family and God stand strongly beside me, I feel so alone. I do not think I've ever in my entire life felt so sad and so alone. I know this is the devil making me feel this way and I must be strong and fight against it.

"Dear God, please help me win this battle. I know every sign you have sent me has been a positive message. Will you send me a clear message tonight? IS there hope for my marriage and my love to return?" I then turn to the Bible and find the following readings open to me:

"What then will the owner of the vineyard do? He will come, put the tenants to death, and give the vineyard to others... Have you not read this scripture passage 'The stone that the builders rejected has become the cornerstone; by the Lord has this been done, and it is wonderful in our eyes.' (Mark 12:1-12).

"Therefore, I tell you, all that you ask for in prayer, believe that you will receive it and it shall be yours" (Mark 11: 24).

"When you stand to pray, forgive anyone against whom you have a grievance so that your heavenly Father may in turn forgive you your transgressions" (Mark 11:25).

At first, I read this and did not understand how it could apply to me. I have prayed for my family to heal. Does this say I will lead them to faith? The tenants are the ones who did wrong. Will God make them "go away" from our situation? I know this does mean that I must pray and have faith to believe that my prayers will be answered. I must banish fear from my mind and from my being. I have already prayed for the woman that took my husband away from me… I have not yet forgiven her. Tonight, I will try. I know that I should not judge her, lest I be judged. I should forgive her so I can be forgiven.

The readings seem to be telling me the steps to take.

1. Believe in my prayers.
2. Forgive.
3. The vineyard will be given to others more deserving. (That is me, right? Am I the vineyard in this scenario?)
4. Become the cornerstone. (Try to lead others to faith.)

Could it be any clearer in direction than that? It really appears as if it is a step-by-step direction guide for me!

It is always darkest before the dawn. I think my tears and despair of earlier in this writing tonight are the evil's wages against me for showing such hope yesterday. I feel better now. I know Jesus carries me, God provides for me, and the Holy Spirit fills my heart with hope, strength, courage, and love!

5

Livin' the Dreams

The next morning, I awake with a renewed resolve to put God first in my faith. The bright sunlight that manages to peak through my windows warms my heart with the thought that He will provide for me and for us... As if on some celestial wavelength, my mother-in-law calls me today. There is a catch in her tone that I pick up on right away. I do not think this call has good news attached to it.

She tells me my husband told her "he wasn't going to do what she wanted him to do." At that moment I am guessing that is referring to me and coming home. She confirms as much. I asked her how did she respond to that? She said, "I said, okay good talking to you. I gotta go now. And then I hung up the phone."

I had to smile at my mother-in-law's strength and candor, despite my own personal heartbreak. When she believed in something, she stood her ground wholeheartedly. I hated to be the subject of the split between her and her beloved son's relationship; I never wanted that, I had always admired their closeness and loving bond.

I wanted to think that my husband had only said that to his mother in an effort to get her to talk to him about the situation and he could argue it out with her or have her convince him to do the opposite of what he was saying he wanted to do. He liked to subscribe to the reverse psychology method of making sense sometimes. Maybe it would be a good thing for all of us to try backing away from him and not continuing to try and force our opinions on him. We should let him try to convince himself instead of us fighting him. Maybe when we all stop fighting him, he will stop wanting the wrong thing and come back to us. Because at this point, he has walked away from his whole family and me. He is not talking or spending any real time with his mom, dad, or brother. The only person he is communicating with is her—the woman he left me for.

Tonight, I pray for the ability to let it go and get out of God's way. Surely, with God at the wheel He will drive us back home to each other. I find solace in the words from 1Timothy 6 verses 17-21. "Don't rely on so uncertain a thing as wealth. RELY ON GOD, who richly provides us with all things for our enjoyment...Guard what has been entrusted to you...Grace be with all of you."

When I go through the steps of Lectio Divina, which is a process of reading the Bible and then rereading the passage to look for and absorb special meaning to the reader, the words that stand out to me this night are really the "rely on GOD" words. This is exactly what I was trying to say to myself earlier! I need to get out of God's way and just trust in Him! The words that come to my mind next are from part of the prayer to the sacred heart of Jesus: Sacred Heart of Jesus, I trust in you!

(For those not familiar with this prayer, a version is included below.)

The Prayer to the Sacred Heart
Oh Lord Jesus Christ, to Your most Sacred Heart
I confide this intention {name petition}.
Only look upon me, then do what Your love inspires.
Let Your Sacred Heart decide. I count on You.
I trust in You. I throw myself on Your mercy.
Lord Jesus, You will not fail me.

Sacred Heart of Jesus, I trust in You. Sacred Heart
of Jesus, I believe in Your love for me.
Sacred Heart of Jesus, Your kingdom come. Sacred
Heart of Jesus, I have asked You for many favors,
but I earnestly implore this one. Take it,
place it in Your open Heart.
When the Eternal Father looks upon it, He will
see it covered with Your Precious Blood.
It will be no longer my prayer, but Yours, Jesus.
Sacred Heart of Jesus, I place all my trust in You.
Let me not be disappointed. Amen.

Over the course of the next several nights I dream that my husband
and I get back together. I dreamt that we got remarried. My mom had
a dream the same exact night. In her dream, my husband had created a
new list of things to do and on the top of that list was circled: Get back
together with Cecilia. That night when I read from the Bible, I opened
the pages to the battle scene between David and Goliath. This is where
David defeats the giant Goliath in God's name with a tiny pebble and a
slingshot. "All this multitude, too, shall learn that it is not by sword or
spear that the Lord saves. For the battle is the Lord's, and he shall deliver
you into our hands" (1Samuel 17:38-58). Again, this reminds me to trust
and rely on God in my journey and battle through this turmoil.

The entry into my journal on January eighteeth reveals that I dreamt
the very next night again of reuniting with my husband. This dream is
not remembered as clearly when I wake, but there was a sense of some
baby talk or blessing there within the reunion. I know I woke up from the
dream feeling hopeful and happy. As I prayed this night, tears streamed
down my face. The tears were not overwhelmingly sad as they had been
in the past; they for some reason felt as if they had a cleansing quality to
them. I gathered my strength and opened my bible. The first words I see
jump off the page! "HE CAME HOME" (Mark 3:20).

I continue reading, gathering speed, and feeling as if on the verge of a breakthrough in my findings. From verse 20 through chapter 4 and beyond in this section of Mark, the gospel describes many miracles that Jesus performed. Mark 3:23-30 deals specifically with Jesus being accused of having an unclean spirit and again in Mark 5:1-20 where Jesus casts out a demon in the man of Gerasenes. I read this as verification that my earlier suspicions may have been founded in fact. I from the beginning felt my fight in my marriage was against evil and the wage against the family. I felt I was battling pure evil and did not understand how my precious love had turned into this unreachable, cold-hearted man that was unwilling to communicate even basic words with me. Surely what I was reading tonight was confirmation that Jesus and I were battling on the same front. Perhaps we were on the edge of a breakthrough here? Maybe that is why my tears felt more like a cleanse than like the usual tears of my broken heart.

"Please God, hear my prayers and allow my husband the desire, courage, and faith to come home to me and be the husband that I so desperately need. Please give us the chance to correct our misguided efforts and place you at the center of our marriage and our life."

I find in 2 Samuel 1: 1-16 the words: ...May you be blessed by the Lord for having done this kindness... And now may the Lord be kind and faithful to you. I, too, will be generous to you for having done this." I trust that God has put us on the path to great love. I know in my heart that God wants us to be happy and remain married. I know this period of trial is so that I can be closer to God and fully appreciate all the blessings in my life. I find myself praying even more fervently for my husband and his family. I pray that we will all be able to love God fully, that we will be blessed to know God, and worship Him together at church someday. I would love to bring them all to greater faith, especially if it were through my faith and my Catholic Church. "Sirs, what must I do to be saved? And they said, believe in the Lord Jesus and you and your household will be saved. So, they spoke the word of the Lord to him and to everyone in his house" (Acts 16: 30-32).

It was Martin Luther King, Jr. Day. There was no school. I had another dream of my husband last night. In this dream, we were trying to get back together but it was awkward. It was as if I was walking on eggshells and HE was testing ME to see where I was. Like I was the one with things to prove to him! In the dream, he was not trying to convince me he had changed or improved himself. It was like I was trying to win his approval back instead of the other way around! Surely this dream had to be a result of my subconscious connecting my conscious mind and the conversation my mom and I just had about how we did not think he was ready to come home yet. Either way, this dream rocked my strength. Perhaps because I am impatient. I cried on and off all day today.

In tonight's Lectio Divina, I found Jeremiah 23: 7-8, 28 "Therefore the days will come, says the Lord… They shall again love on their own land… Let the prophet who had a dream recount the dream; let him who has my word speak my word truthfully!" What can this mean?

Sometime the next day, I take the time to mail my husband a check that his grandmother sent to us. Every year she mails us a check for our wedding anniversary and this year was no exception. I did not feel right cashing it myself, or even taking half so I just stuck the whole thing in a different envelope and sent it to him. I understand what her point is; she's trying to recognize the fact that we are still married, and she wishes we would remain that way. It comforted me to know this and that meant more to me than the money.

I also texted him. He had previously cancelled my cable subscription even though I was paying for all the bills. Four car payments, the house, all the insurance, taxes, a boat, all utilities, and everything was getting paid by me but since this bill was in his name, he cancelled the service. I texted him to tell him they had not sent me the box to return the satellite receiver and if he didn't want to be charged the $300 for non-returned equipment, he should take care of it. Petty, I know, but a girl has her limits. He managed to text me back right away this day; very politely, "Thank you. I'll call them."

Call me stupid, but I took that small act as a good sign. I went ahead and reserved our normal camping sites for the spring and summer season. God willing, I hoped we would be back together by then.

This night, another dream came of my husband and I getting back together. As usual, I don't recall all the details, but only that we were talking and working things out. We were on separate boats at The Lake. Someone dove off or fell from my boat and resurfaced to climb onto his. The people in the dream were saying that this is a sign that someone is about to die. This must've scared my husband and me because we started talking. We ended up kissing and telling each other how much we loved each other. We said we did not want to lose one another!

I have no idea why I dreamed this, or even what it means. I have concluded that I don't want to dream of him! I always wake anxious even if it is a relatively good dream. This dream was okay, I think... Instead of wasting too much time trying to figure out the dreams, I decided to pour my energy into getting some odd jobs finished around the house. If my husband were coming home, I would show him that I could do some of the things on our "to do" list. I would do them without him and make him proud of the time I had used without him here. I finished painting the bathroom. I still needed to paint the guest bedroom door, the master bedroom door, the closet doors, and all the trim in the bedroom. I will finish all these items before he comes home!

In 2 Chronicles 27:6, I focus on the words, "Thus Jotham continued to grow strong because he lived resolutely in the presence of the Lord, his God." I continue to read on in the same section of the bible that night. A little further down, I draw more comfort from the words, "...Thus the service of the house of the Lord was reestablished... Hezekiah and all the people rejoiced over what God had reestablished for the people, and at how suddenly this had been done" (2 Chronicles 29: 35-36).

Again, the next night another dream comes. I do not know what it was about this time except again we were talking about trying to fix things. Five of the last six nights have led to dreams of my husband. Why such a sudden onslaught? As has become my practice, I open the bible for answers and solace. I turn to Luke 22 and find in verse 32 "I pray that your own faith may not fail…" In verse 40 He tells me: "Pray that you may not undergo the test…Father if you are willing, take this cup away from me; still not my will but yours be done." In verse 51 "…Stop, no more of this!" And finally, in Luke 23 verse 29 "…For indeed, the days are coming when people will say, 'Blessed are the barren, the wombs that never bore and the breasts that never nursed."

When I read these passages back in January 2013, I was perplexed. I knew the story but could not figure out how God was trying to tell me it applied to me. I knew I kept praying for God to give me the Miracle, to give me back my husband and fix my family. But at the same time, I was trying to also accept his will and pray that his will, not mine be done. This reading showed me that even Jesus asked God to save him from his suffering if it was His will. I could also realize that in these passages Jesus was instructing his disciples to pray that they would not be tested. That day, several times, I remember wondering if I was doing wrong by asking God to save our marriage. Was this like Jesus telling his friends to pray that they were not tested? If God saved my marriage and granted me the miracle, would I be tested even further? What was the last line of the passage supposed to mean about people saying being glad about being barren?

6

The Battle Begins

Before opening the bible this night, I prayed that God would make his words and meaning clear to me. I asked that I not just see and interpret what I wanted to see. That last line surely foretells of at some point being glad to not have children with my husband, right? But it also seems to say keep praying that I do not have to go through this awful test!

The next words are a direct entry from my journal. The words alone cannot express the amount of overwhelming comfort and peace that I was permitted to feel during the following experience. It has never or since happened to me, but I think it reveals a particularly important truth about the exact power of God's love. I believe this event shows how his holy family comes down to stand guard around us when we are most in need; even when we do not ourselves know exactly how much we need them.

1-24-13

I kept waking up last night thinking about the Most Holy Virgin Mary, Mother of God. What I mean is, every time I woke up, seemingly for no reason, it felt as if the Virgin Mother was with me. At one time I felt her standing beside me. Another time, I felt her arms wrapped around me in a warm embrace, as if guarding me. There was a tranquility in the air and absolute silence filled with peace.

I told my mother-in-law about this experience when I spoke with her today. I told her about how I felt like people and forces were working on my husband and our situation. She started to cry. She told me she was so happy that I shared this experience with her because she had a terrible nightmare the night before… She shared how her nightmare had scared her awake and how she immediately had started praying. She told me she absolutely believed that Mary had been protecting me and that she was so glad that I was praying and staying strong. She said that me telling her about my experience made her feel safer and stronger. I shared with her that I had this overwhelming sense that we had turned a corner towards good.

The following Bible verses were discovered over several nights of reading and carry special meaning to me as I think they are meant to encourage me as messages from God for the days of battle about to come… I would suggest to the reader perhaps a journaling exercise on any of these verses if you find yourself amid a spiritual or emotional battle where you need God's guidance.

2 Corinthians 7
<u>Verse 3</u> "I do not say this in condemnation, for I have already said that you are in our hearts…"
<u>Verse 4</u> "I have great confidence in you, I have great pride in you; I am filled with encouragement."
<u>Verse 8</u> "For even if I saddened you by my letter, I do not regret it…"
<u>Verse 9</u> "I rejoice now… because you were saddened into repentance; for you were saddened in a godly way, so that you did not suffer loss in anything because of us."
<u>Verse 13</u> "For this reason we are encouraged." "…For the joy of Titus since his spirit has been refreshed by all of you."
<u>Verse 15</u> "And his heart goes out to you all the more, as he remembers the obedience of all of you…"
<u>Verse 16</u> "I rejoice, because I have confidence in you in every respect."

One late evening, I arrive home from work around five p.m. and walk out to the mailbox. Inside is a certified letter. MY HUSBAND IS SUING ME FOR DIVORCE. I find myself unable to breathe. There is literally no air in my lungs as I stand there clutching the envelope in one hand as my eyes keep filling and refilling with tears as I struggle to read the blurred words in front of me. The grounds for divorce that he has filed under are gross neglect, extreme cruelty, and incompatibility. I cannot believe this! The man that I have loved more than anything in this world has signed his name, under penalty of perjury that he believes that I neglected him and was extremely cruel to him? The one that I thought was the LOVE OF MY LIFE believes that we are incompatible?

In the frozen January air, I trudge back to my car and find the focus to put the keys in the ignition. Never in my life had I needed the warmth and compassion of my parents more than I did in this moment. They lived a mere seven miles down the road, but between my shortness of breath and the overflowing stream of tears running down my cheeks, the drive there seems interminable. I do not remember the words that I find to explain this shocking event; I think I just thrusted the envelope of lies in front of them and let them read it for themselves. I watched their own disbelief cloud their faces; my husband was very well respected and loved by my parents. They too thought with all their heart that he would turn himself around and find his way back to me.

That night, feeling just like a puddle of mush, I turned to the Bible for support. I found a repeat conversation. It was 2 Maccabees 12 verses 17-25. This section of the Bible describes in detail the persecution renewed and the activity of Judas when he was fighting for the Jewish people as they were being treated unjustly. I could not help but draw parallels to my own life and how I was feeling treated unfairly by someone I once trusted a great deal. This made it even more relevant and meaningful as to why Mary had her arms wrapped so tightly around me the night before. She was standing by my side and filling my heart with strength that she knew I would need today. I am 100 percent sure that I had I not had that extra boost of love and comfort I would not have felt the tiny bit of strength that I did manage to muster up today. Thank you, Mary!

I woke up the next morning at 5:30 am. I just could not go back to sleep. I called my husband at 6:30 and asked him what exactly had changed in the last 24 days that he now wanted a divorce instead of a dissolution? He replied that he did not think I would agree to a dissolution. I reminded him of our last conversation when I told him I would not file but if he did and he wanted to, we could work it out. I had told him at that time he could have whatever he wanted. I really believed that "other woman" was talking in his ear and convincing him of what he should be doing! They even had the same divorce lawyer for crying out loud!

He then told me that he would call the lawyer on Monday and cancel the divorce and refile for a dissolution. I highly doubt he will do that! I asked him how could he defile my character? He said he did not want to put that in the paperwork, but his lawyer told him to do it. I argued that what he said could not be true because the lawyer worked for him and he signed it. He had to have known how it would hurt me! I told him, up to that day I had not said one bad word about him to anyone and I had not. I told him that what he was basing this divorce on is a slap in my face! (What a terrible thing he has done to me! He has done nothing but hurt me for the last eight months.)

My real husband is <u>dead.</u> This man is not my husband. My real husband was loving, caring, honorable, trustworthy, and of solid, moral character. The man I knew and loved has to have died. I am a widow. I will always love the man I married. I must bury him and let the dirt pile on top. *I am devastated.* Completely, utterly, and whole-heartedly broken. My marriage is over.

Tonight, when I turn to the Bible, I am quite amazed when the following passages pop out at me. Remember, I do not go looking for certain scriptures to read. I am opening the good Book and letting the pages find me. This is what the Holy Spirit tells me tonight through 1 Corinthians 7 verse 15 *"If the unbeliever separates, however, let him separate. The brother or sister is not bound in such cases; God has called you to peace. For how do you know, wife whether you will save your husband; or how do you know, husband, whether you will save your wife?"*

I read this again and again, astonished that such a clear and meaningful message has been laid out for me specifically on this day. My heart still aches of course, but God is calling me to try and find peace. God knows from the very beginning I felt called to save my husband. I wanted so much to bring him to Jesus and for us to live the Catholic life together. I do thank God that he was able to go through RCIA and to be baptized. For a short time, we were able to enjoy going to church together. That Easter vigil mass I was so proud of him and his new beginning in the Church! If nothing else, his soul was cleansed through baptism and he was confirmed in the church that same day! I did try my best to save my Love and bring him towards heaven.

Two days later, I went to see my husband. He did not know I was coming; I just showed up at his work. We talked for 30 minutes. Well, mostly I talked, and he listened. I think we can do a dissolution if he is telling the truth about being willing to sit down with me on Wednesday and sort things out. God help me, I still love him-- or the man he was when we married. I still pray that God will bring my real husband back.

When I turn to my Bible that night, I find Sirach waiting for me. The reading is certainly about trials and being tested, but it is not that God is testing us. It is that others test us, or we test ourselves, or that life tests our courage, or our faith and God is here to support us. I find through this reading God is supporting me and will continue to help me through this crisis.

Sirach 2:1-18
V1 "…When you come to serve the Lord, prepare yourself for trials."
V5 "For in fire gold is tested, and worthy men in the crucible of humiliation."
V9 "You who fear the Lord, hope for good things, for lasting joy and mercy."

V10 "…Has anyone hoped in the Lord and been disappointed?"
V18 "For equal to his majesty is the mercy that he shows."

The very next day, I talked to my husband again. And then I yelled some too. He would not change the papers he filed until we agree on the terms of the dissolution. We are meeting tomorrow night to go over them. I asked him to please let my husband speak to me one last time. He said, "yesterday was the most he's seen of him in a long time." Isn't that weird? That he would acknowledge my reference to seeming like it is two people inside of him? He spoke about himself in the third person. I think again if only he could be convinced to seek treatment… Luke 23 verse 18 says, "Away with this man! Crucify him! Crucify him!" When I saw that verse, it was like how I felt towards my husband: whoever he was, or pretending to be, I wanted him far away from me.

The day of reckoning is here. My husband and I met at the local Amvets for almost two hours tonight. It was calm, informative, agreeable, and heartbreaking all at the same time. I agreed to all his "demands" and asked him to take out the lies about gross neglect and extreme cruelty. He agreed. I still love him and saw the man I married in him tonight. I still wish/pray/hope that God could fix us and perform a miracle! But maybe he has a better plan for us. I know he loves us both more than we could ever love each other, so it is best that we just wait and see what is in store for us. Tonight, the Bible tells me: …This sign shall take place tomorrow and We must go a three days' journey in the desert… Exodus 8:19, 23.

I could not get out of bed to go to work today. It is near the end of January. I am too tired and depressed. The psychiatrist I am seeing says I should take time off and he will write me an excuse; he says I'm under too much stress and suffering from real depression. I do not know if that is true, but I do know that I just want to sleep. Throw the covers over my head and forget about life for a while-- a long while. Can I just do that?

Instead, I haul myself up at some point around 4:00 and go to talk to a lawyer about divorce. I am contesting the divorce, based on the grounds that my husband filed, but will agree to his settlement terms. My lawyer is suggesting marriage counselling too. I am sure that'll go over like a lead balloon with my husband. I am still praying for the miracle but trusting more and more in God's plan. My emotions are so haywire and all over the place!

As I opened up the Bible tonight, I asked God what he wanted to tell me today besides, "Stop making me repeat myself!" I laughed out loud! Sorry! Sometimes I need to hear things over and over. I opened the book to Mark 3:20. "HE CAME HOME." I burst out laughing! God already showed me this line on January eighteeth. He IS repeating himself to me! This was the first line that I touched and read again tonight. I started crying at this point. It reminded me of the interior voice that I heard back in October that told me to stop crying. Back then I heard, "Stop crying, Cecilia. He's gonna come back."

Mark 3:20 also says, "He came home…when his relatives heard this, they set out to seize him, for they said, "He is out of his mind." The scribes who had come from Jerusalem said, "He is possessed by Beelzebul," This is the same thought that I had the other day, that my husband wasn't in his right mind. That maybe he was bipolar or suffering from some mid-life crisis or something. Or remember way back when I first thought my marriage was under attack by the forces of evil? I believe that is what this passage is telling me now. I know there is more at work in our fight here than just a normal marriage separation. I do not believe that the kind of love we shared just disintegrates seemingly overnight.

7

❧

A Billboard Sign

My mother told me today that she thinks I should go forward with pursuing an annulment in the church. She said if I do that it will be over and done with and then if I find someone else nothing would stand in my way of getting remarried and I would not lose any time. I just cannot say that I believe that my marriage was a mistake. I promised 'til death do us part. Another marriage and babies could be possible for me; I am not too old. But that is of this world. I promised to God and to my husband that I would only marry once. Maybe I am supposed to keep my promise and stay married in the church even if he is not. He could still come home! Even if our local judge grants us a civil divorce, God has not said that. (Yet.)

Today I struggled to get out of bed again. It took me an hour and a half! I received an email from Saint Andrew's Church in Porter from their marriage ministry that they would pray for me and my husband this Saturday during their marriage prayer-a-thon. They told me to hope because God can do all things! I am very thankful that we are in their prayers. I even signed up to pray for another couple in need during this day of prayer. I thought if someone else was praying for us then I would return the favor and pray for another couple in need.

My husband's Grandmother sent me a letter saying she loves me. She said she prays for me and for my husband every day. I am so thankful for that too! Please, God. Save our marriage!

2 Kings 2:19-22 "...The water is bad and the land unfruitful...thus says the Lord, " I have purified this water. Never again shall death or miscarriage spring from it." And the water has stayed pure even to this day, just as Elisha prophesied."

After I read from the Bible tonight, Father Michael from Saint Andrew's Church in Porter called. He said he read my request from the prayers in the Marriage Ministry and wanted to reach out to me and my husband to offer a meeting. He said maybe we could talk, and it would at least help my husband with all the anger he has stored up inside. I explained that I did not hold out much hope that he would be interested. Father Michael told me to tell my husband that since he is a Christian, he should at least try everything. I agreed. Father Michael then encouraged me to get involved with one of the women's faith sharing groups they have at the parish. He said if I could connect with people during this time of need it could help me. I stop to think for a minute... It is probably a good idea for all of us to have a list of ALL the people in our lives that can help us at any given moment.

I am very scared to ask my husband to meet with Father Michael. He hasn't exactly been really receptive to anything religious lately and I'm afraid he'll say no and I'll be disappointed again. However, I feel like God is throwing us a lifeline here! I shake off my fears and tell myself to call him because I must put myself and my faith out there because I believe it's what God wants me to do.

My mother-in-law still thinks we are going to get back together even though he filed for divorce. I do not know though. Some days I am hopeful, but today I just feel resigned. I know that is my own human weakness to doubt even when God has shown me so many signs—especially recently. I have trust in Jesus. I say to myself: Jesus, I trust in you!

Matthew 11: 25-28 "At that time, Jesus said in reply, "I give praise to you, Father, Lord of heaven and earth, for although you have hidden these things from the wise and the learned you have revealed them to the childlike. Yes, Father, such has been your gracious will…Come to me, all you who labor and are burdened, and I will give you rest." These words give me a feeling of peace and I can sleep comfortably this night. I know when I just trust in God things will be all right.

It takes me two whole days before I muster up the courage to call my husband. I explain everything that Father Michael said to me and everything that he offered to us. I even reminded my husband that Father Michael was the priest that talked to us during our pre-Cana training before we were married, thinking that would make him believe as I did that there was a meaningful and special connection to Father Michael. But my husband said no to the meeting. He was not willing to sit and talk with Father Michael to discuss anything. I am not surprised, but I was hopeful. I felt like God was reaching out to us, but my husband said that if it came through me it was not a sign from God. He said it would have to be something huge like a message on a billboard specifically to him to make him believe it was for him from God.

In this moment I remember thinking, "*I am so sad right now. I feel like I have no hope left in me. The one thing that I loved and cared about more than anything else in this world is gone—for no reason that I can understand. I am sad, disappointed, broken, lost, and teetering on despair. The future is too far away from now. NOW is a terribly dark place that I can't stand to be in.*"

2 Samuel 22: 17-19 "He reached out from on high and grasped me; he drew me out of the deep waters. He rescued me from my mighty enemy, from my foes, who were too powerful for me. They attacked me on my day of calamity, but the Lord came to my support."

The very next day I had to go wedding dress shopping with my beloved younger sister. While I was over the moon ecstatic for her to be so in love and happy, internally I was brimming with anger and rage that I could not shake. In my mind I am bombarded with memories of my own wedding dress shopping and images of my wedding and how happy I was. Tears threaten to spill over throughout the day, and I ride on the verge of sadness, but smile through the pain regardless. I am determined to not be a dark cloud of negativity when my sister deserves all the happiness the world can give her! Despite how difficult these circumstances are that I am in, this moment is hers and I will not allow it to be tarnished. I pray in my mind a prayer I crafted one day while I was similarly lost in my own inner turmoil:

I pray for wisdom so that I can do the right thing when presented with an opportunity to decide. I pray for courage to face each day. I pray for strength to do the best I can in every situation I am faced with. I pray for faith so I can remain focused. I pray for peace so that I can remain calm. I pray for love to remain so that anger cannot enter. I pray for clarity so that I do not get sidetracked on details that are not important. I pray that not my will, God's will be done. Amen.

Later that night I return to the Bible and read from Matthew 20: 30-34. "Two blind men... cried out, "Lord, Son of David, have pity on us!... Jesus stopped and called them and said, "What do you want me to do for you?" They answered him, "Lord, let our eyes be opened." Moved with pity, Jesus touched their eyes. Immediately they received their sight and followed him."

I asked God tonight to give my husband a sign so obvious and so large that he couldn't help but to see it and know that it was from God and to know that he is to turn back to God, family, and himself. My husband told me the night before when I spoke with him that he wouldn't walk back to the church unless God gave him a sign so obvious and so big that he couldn't ignore it and he would know it had to be for him. I prayed that my husband's eyes would be opened and that he would follow God. I did not want anything bad or hurtful to happen, I just wanted my husband healed. I know God can do all things. "Whatever you ask for in faith, you will receive" (Mark 21:22). I asked for my husband back: healed, repentant, ready for love, and for God.

8

Thy Will Be Done

I probably should take my doctor up on his offer to take some time off work. I just could not force myself to get up out of bed and face the day today. It is too much. It is like an overwhelming force is weighing on me, sitting on top of my chest and forcing me to stay in bed. My head knows I should get up and get the day started and my heart wants to feel better and move forward but some force larger than myself keeps me rooted in place some days.

I did manage at some point in the afternoon to go into the library to pay some bills online. (I had canceled my internet to cut down on costs since I was now paying for everything on my own.) There was this guy sitting next to me on the computer surfing the internet through a bunch of different online dating websites. He started talking to me telling me about how many different dates he could get online and how his last three girlfriends had come from online sources. No offense, but I thought to myself: *if this guy could get dates, surely, I could find someone to love me if my husband didn't want me anymore!* I finished up paying my bills and joined plentyoffish.com. It had worked for my sister and a few other people I knew! What was the harm?

I quickly realized online dating was for the birds! It is so time consuming. I must be too picky or something, because even though I quickly got messages of interest I did not see anyone that I wanted to meet. It did make me feel a little better though, because men on there were quick to tell me I was pretty. In my current state of mind, I sure needed that! Despite those compliments, I still asked God to save our marriage that night in my prayers. I guess I am just not over my husband. I read from the Bible in Psalm 12:6-7 "Because they rob the weak, and the needy groan, I will now arise," says the Lord; "I will grant safety to whoever longs for it." The promises of the Lord are sure...."

I have started to investigate bipolar disorder with my husband in mind. We have always thought he might have seasonal affective disorder, but maybe it is more. It truly does seem like he is two different people at times now that this divorce issue has reared its ugly head. It is as if the man I married is still in there somewhere, but he is trapped and cannot get out into the light of day. He is overwhelmed by this angry and distraught man who will not talk or deal with issues in a calm and rational way. I am not looking for excuses, just answers.

Dear God, should I just give up? Matthew 26:50 "Friend, do what you have come for." Matthew 26:54 "It must come to pass in this way." Matthew 26:56 "But all this has come to pass that the writings of the prophets may be fulfilled."

Today is February 7, 2013. I am praying the rosary with Mother Angelica on EWTN. I know some may call me crazy and say that I must not know when to give up, but I keep getting these thoughts in my head as I pray:

- Father Amobi, whose name means "who knows the heart of man", telling me not to worry, that he knew my husband a little bit and that he believed my husband will come back...
- That interior voice telling me to stop crying because my husband will come back...
- The line of the rosary when we say, "After this our exile..."

- An overall feeling of peace that my husband will come to his senses and want to fix things…

Dear God, your messages to me have been positive and uplifting. Thank you. Please heal my husband and send him home. I will take care of him, his family, and love them the way of your will. Amen.

Before I turned to the Bible, I asked God again to please don't make me give up my husband and my marriage. I asked that my husband be sent back to me renewed so that we might live with God at the center of our lives and to give us another chance. I turned to 2 Kings 4: 14, 16, 36, 37 "Can something be done for her?… This time next year you will be fondling a baby son… Take your son… She came in and fell at his feet in gratitude…"

I quickly started doing the math; this was how literal I was taking my Bible readings! If my husband came back now, I could get pregnant, so that a year from now we could have a baby in our arms! I thought for sure this was a clear sign that my prayers were being answered and that my husband was coming back to me. How could it mean any other thing?

As elated as I was the day before by the "possibilities" of a reconciliation with my husband and the potential of a baby being the ultimate gift to our marriage, the following day brings more emotional doubt, misgivings, and worry. My emotions have been up and down like a roller coaster from day one. I seem to find myself hopeful one moment then wallowing in pits of despair the next. The Holy Spirit uplifts me through prayer on a nightly basis and I have this wonderful feeling that my prayers are being heard and that I am in true communication with God. For some strange reason, the mornings are hard. It is like I must start all over each morning and muster up the courage to keep going on my own and trust that Jesus will keep carrying me through this storm. Like when he helped Peter walk on water if he kept his eyes on Jesus. That is what I have to do: Keep Jesus in my sight. I know this is a battle between good and evil and in the year of marriage I am purposefully battling it out in a desperate attempt to duct tape my relationship and love back together with absolutely no support, conversation, or string of hope given to me from my husband.

My mother in law shared with me a dream she had. She dreamt she was face to face with Jesus and she could see his radiance and all the light surrounding him. She described how beautiful he was and when he smiled at her she felt such love and warmth. Then, in an instant her dream turned to a nightmare as the smile changed to a grin and the face turned into the nasty, evil face of the devil and he leered at her. My mother in law told me she awoke with a start, her heart pounding fiercely in her chest.

She asked me what I thought it meant. I thought I knew right away. I said it represented the struggle between good and evil, plain as day. She had been leaning on God for support and love and had been praying so heavily since my marriage suddenly imploded. I told her the devil did not like it. I told her it was even more reason she couldn't stop now and had to keep praying. What I did not tell her, was that I thought it also meant that we must be making progress with our prayers.

I prayed to God to give me the wisdom to realize if I should give up on my husband and for the strength to be able to do just that if it was His will. I also asked that God's word be understood by me according to what He wanted me to know, understand, or think about. I did not want to interpret anything based on my own desires or to think that something was coming from God only because the words I was reading were what I wanted to hear. That night I found the words from Mark 4: 11, 20. "The mystery of the kingdom of God has been granted to you. But to those outside everything comes in parables...But those sown on rich soil are the ones who hear the word and accept it and bear fruit thirty and sixty and a hundred-fold."

I wake up the next Saturday and feel the happiest and content that I have felt in a long time. There is no real reason or source of my contentment, just an overall sense of peace. I am considering what shall be my sacrifice for the Lenten season. I think I am being called to give up my longing for my husband during these 40 days. Lent starts this coming Wednesday; maybe if I am able to give up my longing and my desire for him, after 40 days I'll either be over him or God will have worked His miracle. By that time, I will have also completed my prayer to St. Therese of the Little Flower. (I am supposed to receive a rose from heaven...) Dear God, lead me in the direction of your will. "And since the Lord does not consider this enough, he will also deliver Moab into your grasp" (2 Kings 3:18). I admit, I do not know what this reading means to me personally or how it applies to me.

Again, I turn to the prayer I wrote a while ago and it gives me a sense of purpose and direction in my days ahead:

I pray for wisdom to do the right thing when
presented with an opportunity to decide.
I pray for courage to face each day.
I pray for strength to do the best I can in every situation I am faced with.
I pray for faith so I can remain focused.
I pray for peace so that I can remain calm.
I pray for love to remain so that anger cannot enter.
I pray for clarity so that I do not get sidetracked
on details that are not important.
Not my will, God's will.
Please allow Your will be done.
Thy will be done.
Amen.

9

A Flash of Emotion

February 10, 2013 was World Marriage Day. The date seems significant to me because every time I turn around events in my life seem to be circling around numbers and dates. My husband and I agreed to meet tomorrow after work. He does not know it's World Marriage Day when we decided this, but I take it as a good sign. I have decided I am going to talk to him about the taxes, a timeline for this divorce, if he will watch our dog when I go on vacation, how I believe he may be suffering from bipolar disorder, and how this nonsense is affecting his parents' health and mine. I know it's a tall order of items to discuss when we have barely been speaking to each other, but I'm going to get it all out in the opportunity I've been given. What do I have to lose? He cannot serve me with divorce papers twice!

I am actually incredibly surprised that he has even agreed to meet me. I wonder if he is even aware of the devastation that his actions have been causing his family. His mom told me her blood pressure was 203/178 today just thinking about him. His dad had to take a nitroglycerin pill last week when he found out under what grounds my husband filed for divorce. This is tearing our family apart and, in my opinion, he doesn't seem to care! I need to make him realize that his actions have repercussions for more than just us and that he needs to care about the promise he made. "To have and to hold, from this day forward, until death do us part…" I pray to God that my husband's eyes will be opened before it is too late! Dear God, please keep him and his family safe and healthy. Please restore their happiness.

At the same time, my mind swirls with conflicting thoughts. I am hopeful because I still love my husband, but I keep thinking that I am being called to give up my husband now, for my Lenten sacrifice. Dear God, please tell me if this is what you desire. I begin to cry and speak to God about my fears about divorce and annulment. How can I believe my marriage was not blessed? I believed that my marriage was to be for the rest of my life, civil divorce or not. Was it my plight to be alone and miserably lonely? I told God I would give up my husband for 40 days or forever, whichever is His will. At the same time, I was silently pleading to Him: Please do not make me do it for my whole life! I begged God to give me an answer.

During prayer, I opened my Bible without direction. Page 1089 in my Bible, Mark 16 right after verse 20 became apparent: My eyes closed, my finger randomly pointed to this: THE SHORTER ENDING. Of course, this makes me happy as I think this means I am not meant to give up my husband for my whole life! Then I immediately begin to double-think it. What if the shorter ending means it is over now? Like it is already over, so it is shorter? I am so confused. I know I am not supposed to worry and just trust in God's plan. I know it does not seem like it, but I am trying to do just that!

My eyes then turned upward on the page and read these lines from Mark 16:18 "They will pick up serpents (with their hands), and if they drink any deadly thing, it will not harm them. They will lay hands on the sick, and they will recover." I reread these lines, at first, they sound scary to me: talking about serpents and drinking deadly things. Then I ponder further and conclude that these lines are telling me that even amid these dangerous, scary possibilities the subject in these verses is not being harmed. I conclude that the message to me is clear: I will not be harmed.

Even though I feel hurt and extremely near danger in this situation, like my heart is breaking and everything I hold near and dear is dying, God is telling me I am going to be ok. Dear God, thank you for listening to me and for answering my cries and my prayers. I will do your will.

It is funny how I can go from hopeful to despair to fear to anger and back to love all in the span of 24 hours. I met with my husband today at 5 p.m. I felt so anxious! If I would have had Xanax, I for sure would have swallowed one. It was that bad! This man I knew so well and loved so much now instilled such a feeling of unknown in me, my emotions were overwhelming.

We started off fine, talking small talk about the dog, taxes, and minutia details of divorce timelines. The meeting seemed overall to be forced, almost clipped. When I broached the subject of bipolar disorder and how it was a cousin to ADHD and seasonal affective disorder he listened attentively, thanked me for trying to think outside the box for what might be wrong with him, and said he might talk about it with his doctor. When we walked out to our cars, he stood outside my driver's side door and hesitated just a moment. I saw a flash of emotion behind his eyes, my heart skipped a beat because I saw his inner turmoil in action and thought maybe he was going to say some lovely words of encouragement like MY husband used to all those years we spent together. Then he purposely set his jaw in place, removed his hand from my car door, and told me good-bye.

That was one of a handful of moments where I knew that the man I had married was still alive inside that shell of a man that was going through the motions of a life before us. It was so hard for me to drive away that day, I wanted to stay and fight! Keep talking to him, knock the sense back into him, make him remember all the good times we had, reconnect our love that had somehow gotten confused and twisted. Instead I drove away, with more tears streaming down my cheeks, knowing I had resolved myself to sacrifice my attachments to this man in order for God's will to take place.

That night my Bible reading was even more confusing to me as I read from 1 Samuel 26:21-25. "Then Saul said: "I have done wrong. Come back, my son, David, I will not harm you again, because you have held my life precious today. Indeed, I have been a fool and have made a serious mistake... Blessed are you, my son David! You shall certainly succeed in whatever you undertake." David went his way, and Saul returned to his home.

Did this reading mean that I was supposed to fight for my husband? That today was in fact a glimmer of hope that meant I was not supposed to step back and give him space? Was it NOT God's will for me to sacrifice my feelings? I did not want to step back, but all the fighting and talking that I had done up to this point had done no good at all. It had only seemed to push him away further into his own resolve to end our marriage. Or was this reading confirmation that my husband and I were indeed supposed to go our separate ways like David and Saul?

The next day is my mother-in-law's birthday. I offer prayers that my husband is a good son to her today. Their relationship has been on the rocks ever since she "sided" with me in the announcement of the separation and pending divorce. She has tried many times to talk him into trying to talk to me and work things out, or to come home but it seems like the more people push or pledge their allegiance to me, the angrier he gets and the further he digs his heels into his own decisions. I continue my prayers this day to include that God will choose to save our marriage and my husband will choose to do God's will. The words, "Jesus, I trust in You..." become almost like a mantra in my mind.

My readings today come from 2 Maccabees 6 verses 12-17. "...Do not be disheartened by these misfortunes... It is in fact, a sign of great kindness to punish sinners promptly instead of letting them go for long... He never withdraws his mercy from us. Although he disciplines us with misfortunes, he does not abandon his own people."

I feel as if I have been blessed with God's grace in these moments. For some reason He has seen me worthy to share these wonderful conversations. He has allowed me to feel inspired and Holy, and like a treasured daughter of God. I never knew before that He loved me so much. My heart has never been so open to the touch of God before and I am so grateful, despite my earthly heartache, that He has entered my door when I asked Him to come in.

47

10

The First Miracle

On February 14, 2013 what I would consider to be the first miracle took place. Remember, this whole time, I have been praying for the miracle, begging God to fix my family. Days earlier I had begun a brief novena to St. Therese of Lisieux, otherwise known as Saint Therese the Little Flower. Upon praying this five-day novena, one should expect a rose from heaven to signify that the prayers are heard, or that the message is received with love.

> O Little Therese of the Child Jesus,
> Please pick a rose for me
> From the heavenly gardens
> And send it to me
> As a message of love.
> O little flower of Jesus,
> Ask God today to grant the favors
> I now place with confidence
> In your hands.
> *(Mention your specific requests)*
> St. Therese,

help me to always believe,
As you did,
In God's great love for me,
So that I might imitate your
"Little Way" each day. Amen

Valentine's Day 2013 was upon us. I was dreading going into work today like never before. Working in a school the office would be a revolving door of candy, flowers, and balloons all day long. In the ten years past I had been able to enjoy this day, knowing my husband loved me and feeling certain some small token of love would be presented or sent to me to represent this Hallmark holiday. This year was different. With absolutely no chance of receiving any mementos of love having already been served with divorce papers only one month prior, I mustered up my courage and made my way to work despite my trepidation.

I walked into the elementary school office to find two little students standing there waiting for me. "Happy Valentine's Day, Mrs. Esther!" they chirped with cute little second and third grade smiles on their faces. At the same time, they pushed forward a beautiful glass vase filled with red silk roses, sparkling ribbons, and a mini-shiny balloon. I took it from them while shocked, happy tears overflowed from my eyes and their little cherub arms encircled my body. Their mother stood there beaming and explained to me that they had just gotten it in their heads to make that for me.

The kicker in this story is that this brother and sister's names are two names that are incredibly special to me. Especially meaningful to me as I have found comfort in the verse Jeremiah 29:11 "For I know the plans I have for you, says the Lord…plans for a future and a hope…" and of course Elizabeth being advanced in age before she was graced with giving birth to John the Baptist.

A short while later, the only other Jeremiah in the entire school walked into the office and asked to see me. In his hand he held a pink box. Inside this box was a red, foil-wrapped chocolate rose. Another rose! I think to myself; God is making sure I am hearing this through the Jeremiahs. This cannot be chalked up to chance. Surely this was a sign from God that my prayers were being heard. Thank you for helping me pray, St. Therese Lisieux.

That night during my prayers and Bible readings I am shown these from 1 Samuel 25 verses 27, 28, 35. "Accept this present, then…and there is no evil to be found in you your whole life long…Go up to your home in peace! See, I have granted your request as a personal favor." I tell you, dear reader, that I did not go searching through the Bible to find specific sections of the text that would suit my purpose here. This selection was discovered on February 14, 2013 the very day that this miracle happened to me! I simply thumbed through the Bible with my eyes closed asking God to tell me what he wants me to know. As I am not a Bible scholar or theologian, I do not know my scriptures well enough to tell you where to find such passages if we were to hunt for them. I genuinely believe that the Holy Spirit blessed me with a conversation, of sorts. And for that, I am incredibly grateful.

I have started to believe once again, that the miracle could really take place. My heart has been in such a place of despair that I had been doubting that my life could ever return to normal. I had prayed for my husband to return and for my family to return to its original state of peace. I wanted my life back!

However, on the very next day, I went out on a date with a guy I met through match.com. He was nice, but short and not really my style. I was also talking to another guy through a dating website, but he seemed moody; and yet a third guy seemed a little interesting because he spoke Spanish, but he didn't talk too much. I thought to myself, why was I trying to date? What was I trying to prove? None of them, I decided, held a candle to my actual husband and so I would wait for God's plan to unfold.

That night the Bible verse that found me was from Titus, chapter 1 verses 5-6. "For this reason I left you in Crete so that might set right what remains to be done and appoint presbyters in every town, as I directed you, on condition that a man be blameless, married only once, with believing children who are not accused of licentiousness or rebellious."

Reading this passage, I decide I must continue to be faithful and graceful so that others can learn from my example, no matter how hard it may be for me. I must remain calm and try to not to grow angry but instead to share my story with others that will listen and perhaps learn. There is still so much of this miracle left to be played out.

At times, it is almost like there is a wall that has been erected around my heart. I have been praying so much, you know. The pain is real and hurts so much but I have agreed to "give up my husband" during this Lenten season. Except for prayer, I still pray for him every day, I just do not long for him, or wish for the past, or cry about why right now. At least that is my goal: to live each day trusting in God's plan. I almost think God placed this wall around my heart right now so I can feel numb to continue to put one foot in front of the other. Like when Peter stepped out of the boat in the sea and walked toward Jesus. If his eyes were on Jesus the raging sea did not bother him and he continued his path. That is how I feel. I can only hope that God continues to work through me and fill me with grace.

2 Samuel 22:17-- "He reached out from on high and grasped me; he drew me out of deep waters. He rescued me from my mighty enemy, from my foes, who were too powerful for me. They attacked me on my day of calamity, but the Lord came to my support." This "Song of Thanksgiving" about God's intervention on David's behalf was shown to me through my daily Bible readings. This was the day that I was to begin my first dose of anti-depressant medication, prescribed by my doctor because of all the stress I was under due to the pending divorce and such. I was not crying, which was good, but it didn't feel normal either. I felt numb—even before the medication took hold. I believe it was because of God's rescue. It must have been what I needed at that moment.

There is a place in the Bible, I remember reading it early on in this struggle, that talks about putting on the full armor of God. I always think about it when I am gearing up for a tough day or even when I am remembering what it felt like for me to go through these struggles back during this time. I imagine myself like Joan of Arc and physically putting on a heavy metal breastplate to protect myself during battle, and arm or shoulder protections as if I were readying for strikes from a powerful sword. On February seventeenth I invited all my friends over for a poker party at my house. This was something that should have been especially difficult because that was an activity that my husband and I used to host together quite frequently. That was like, "our thing." Our house was the poker party place. I know readying the house for this party should have bothered me this day, but it did not. It felt a little like I was outside of what was happening, but a little like I was moving on at the same time. I think now, that feeling of what should have hurt me but not mattering came from God.

I remember praying: Dear God, I hope and pray for your plan to take place. Please heal our hearts, but do not let me grow distant from you. Right now, I feel so tired, but I know you hold us in your arms and care for us. Jesus, I trust in you. And my bible verse from that day was 2 Corinthians 2 verse 4: "…Who encourages us in our every affliction, so that we may be able to encourage those who are in any affliction with the encouragement with which we ourselves are encouraged by God."

Reading those words from Corinthians makes me believe that my task is to continue to encourage others through my example. People seem to be encouraged when I talk to them sometimes. I think that at times, God speaks THROUGH me. When I look back at what I said, I often cannot remember exactly what was said sometimes. I do wish my husband would listen to me, or rather, that he would listen to God. My hope is that SOMEDAY he will listen to God.

I know God has a purpose for my life and I do not believe that I am supposed to be alone. I do not believe that I am even supposed to be mediocre. I do not know what that means, or even what the plan is yet.

Exactly six months before my 40th birthday, I let my mom in on the secret I was keeping to myself: the secret of the first miracle. This is the day I share with my mother the events that happened on Valentine's Day with the roses and Teresa of the Little Flower novena coming true. I have to say, she looked the perfect mixture of shocked, scared, and impressed all rolled into one face! It was amazing to me too. This is the first day that I had the thought of translating this story into a book or sharing it at a conference somehow. Of course, I have no idea how to make that happen, but that night the Holy Spirit tells me in scripture, "With the help of Heaven for our support, we have been saved from our enemies, and they have been humbled...and we have sent them...to renew our former friendship and alliance with them... We have also ordered them to come to you and greet you..." 1 Maccabees 12:15-17.

11

Forged by Fire

As had often happened during this battling time, after a day that I would consider a victory (feeling strong enough to be sharing the miracle of the roses with my mom), the next day I find myself in somewhat of a funk. I felt empty, tired, and distant from what I would normally care about. I lacked energy and determination. All I could do was pray: Dear God, please continue to watch over and bless our family. Keep us safe from the enemy and let us do your divine will. Please keep us wrapped in your loving arms and protect us...

I passionately believe that on days like that, it was nothing more, aye, nothing less, than purely the evil one trying to get to me. I know I was waged in a deep spiritual battle in those days. He had taken my husband, as that was the year dedicated to marriage by the Pope and I know a major battle is against life and marriage. I had set myself in a firm stance against it and my weapon was prayer.

What wisdom should I consider today Lord? My bible answered me, showing me Sirach 24's "Praise of Wisdom." In verses 18 and 21 it says: "Come to me, all you that yearn for me, and be filled with my fruits; ... He who obeys me will not be put to shame, he who serves me will never fail." This causes me to go back and read the verses before, beginning with verse 1 "With three things I am delighted, for they are pleasing to the Lord and to men: Harmony among brethren, friendship among neighbors, and the mutual love of husband and wife."

When I first read this passage, I was focused on the words love of husband and wife and thought that surely the message was that I was to remain true to my marriage and things would work out. Then I reread the verse and began to think about the word MUTUAL. It had to be the mutual love of husband and wife. I was not clear on what was going on in my husband's mind in these moments, but mutual love sure was not one of them for some reason. But I knew that the former part of this verse was meant to strengthen me. Obey God and I would not feel shame, because in my situation I had not done anything wrong. Also, serve the Lord and I would not fail. The words were meant to be intertwined for me if I could just stay true to them.

Not a day goes by without me thinking of my husband. I still call him my husband too. We are not divorced yet. Even if the state manages to declare us divorced the Catholic Church will have to annul our marriage before I could consider myself unmarried. I pray for him every day but have stopped asking God to save our marriage. God knows what is in my heart. Even me writing this is an admission of my wants. I must trust that God will provide for what I (or we) need. My jaw does hurt though, from clenching in all my tension! Another 40 days will be so hard to do after so many days already. However, I must persevere for the greater good or else God would not ask me to do this.

Tonight "this is the Lord's message" in Zechariah 4:6-14 "Not by an army, nor by might, but by my spirit...you shall know that the Lord of hosts has sent you...He said 'These are the two anointed who stand by the Lord of the whole earth."

I do not know about you, dear reader, but when I read this-even to this day it gives me chills and makes me teary eyed. I feel as if God is speaking to me and telling me that He did anoint us on our wedding day and that our marriage was meant to be. So many times I think it would be easier if I were made of the stuff that would allow me to walk away, build the concrete wall around my feelings and my memories and steel myself against the world to start over. Then I picture myself, standing there on the altar of the church on my wedding day with my husband, thinking the thought that it was he and I against the world that day forevermore. I thought in that moment it was forever. Is it possible that I was so wrong on that day in January 2005 and am again so wrong now as I read this bible verse?

The following day finds me in no real position of advancement as far as my feelings or mental health is concerned. I decide for my meditation I am going to just sit and be quiet and try to hear God whisper to me. 1 Samuel 28:6 "He therefore consulted the Lord; but the Lord gave no answer…" I am taken aback. What?! How can this be? Dear God, do you grow tired of me and my whining, I think? I consult the bible again. This time Zechariah 13:9 "I will bring one-third through fire and I will refine them as silver is refined, and I will test them as gold is tested. They shall call upon my name and I will hear them. I will say, they are my people, and they shall say, the Lord is my God." So, I am thinking I am about to be tested even further.

The very next day proves this to be true. My brother-in-law and I were in constant communication at this point. I think he somehow felt responsible for taking care of me and trying to see me through this time. Maybe because we had grown close over the years, maybe because he was part of the reason his brother and I had met and gotten together in the first place, or perhaps because he simply loved me like a sister, I'm not sure. Regardless, on this day he told me he thought it was finally time for me to give up. Previously when this all started, he told me to hold on for as long as I could! Before, he really thought his brother would come around, that it might take a while but that I should have faith in our love and that he knew his brother—that he would come to his senses and that I shouldn't give up on him if I could just wait long enough. But that day, February 22, he was telling me to walk away and not spend another minute hurting, waiting, or hoping for his brother.

In my opinion, he even seemed a little angry when he said it. Like he himself had lost a little something for his brother recently. He explained to me that he believed that his brother had done something so egregious to our wedding vows and he was not able to own up to it or try to fix it. I asked him if there was another woman. He just looked at me. I told him I already knew that there was, could he just confirm it? Were they living together yet? Had he met her? My brother-in-law just looked at me, unwilling to throw his brother any farther under the bus.

I was shocked. For my brother-in-law to believe this, I had to give it some merit. He would never just say these things without having some real proof, even if he could not share everything with me for fear of overstepping some confidentiality boundary with his brother. But I knew deep down that what he was telling me was big. And I knew it was true—even if I did not want to believe it. And I did not want to believe it—no way!

The man I married would NEVER do that. So many times, we'd been out together and women had tried hitting on him, right in front of me, and he never looked at another woman. There was even a time that he had shared with me a story from his childhood about when he had suspected that his parents were thinking of splitting up and how he had watched his mother become so upset about that situation. He had told me he would NEVER do that to me because he had picked his own mother up off the floor one day when she was so upset.

I was really struggling to reconcile these two truths. I knew my brother-in-law was speaking to me in an absolute truth. Yet, I knew the man that I married was honest and faithful. In my heart I had to hold on to the fact that God could bring us through this trial. Everything in my journal had been telling me to trust in the Lord and that He would save us.

That night I turned to the Bible asking again for reassurance. Please God, tell me again that I am right. Please tell me that you will bring my husband back to me… What I turned to in the bible next would not have been my choice if I were trying to pick out my good thoughts myself, I can assure you. Instead God led me to this: Jeremiah 51:58 "…The walls of spacious Babylon shall be leveled utterly; her lofty gates shall be destroyed by fire. The toil of the nations is for nothing; for the flames, the people weary themselves."

There you have it, I thought. It is finished.

Broken, deserted and utterly alone, the next day I signed up for all the single dating sites I could think of. If my husband could find someone so quickly and change his life, then so could I. I was a strong, independent woman. I was not going to sit at home and cry anymore, wondering when my life was going to get better. I was going to make it happen for myself. I had plenty to offer someone: I was successful, loving, and beautiful. I was a catch! If my husband did not want me, I would find someone that did.

One night, I made plans to meet a man named Matt. We had talked for several days through this messaging app and I was ready to meet in public. There was a college football game that day, so I did not need another reason to get out there. Somehow though, our signals got crossed and we did not end up meeting.... In truth, I chickened out. I was there, in the parking lot, car turned off, about to go inside the wings place, then for some reason I turned the keys in the ignition and drove away instead. I do not know why, I just chickened out.

When I returned home and opened my bible, I discovered why from Luke 2:39. "When they had fulfilled all the prescriptions of the law of the Lord, they returned to Galilee, to their own town of Nazareth." For all my blustering and angry feelings after my brother-in-law's announcement, I knew in my heart I loved my husband and I just was not ready to even talk to another man. No matter if I believed he had cheated on me, I loved him, and I wanted to talk to him and try to find a way to fix whatever had been broken. I wanted him to come home. I knew in the depths of my soul that when I said "I do" at our wedding I meant that I would forever through good times and bad, like we were supposed to, come what may. The problem was in this moment I did not know what else I could do except to sit and wait for the rest of the story to unfold in front of me.

Luke 2:40 says "The child grew and became strong, filled with wisdom; and the favor of God was upon him." During my readings that night I was not sure what that meant. I even wrote in my journal that I had no idea how that reading pertained to me. But sit and wait I would. As I believed I was growing weak, and tears continued to stream down my face on a daily basis, I had nothing else in my plan to do except to wait and see what God's plan would be.

Daily I would break down and cry with shoulders wracking. Often, I wondered how my body continued to produce the salt needed to fuel so many tears. Nightly I prayed to God on my knees. Even during my weakness, I thought I had been presenting myself as strong. I have really tried NOT to be thinking about my situation all the time. I had been trying to block it out. But then in doing that, I worry that I am also unconsciously blocking God's thoughts out. I do not want to do that. It is God's thoughts that are making me stronger! If I listen, I know he will speak to me. The bible tells us 'if at first you hear my voice, harden not your heart.'

Turning to Proverbs 16:1-9, I find a goldmine of inspiration: "Man may make plans in his heart, but what the tongue utters is from the Lord... Entrust your works to the Lord, and your plans will succeed... In his mind a man plans his course, but the Lord directs his steps."

To me, it seems as if this is direct inspiration meant for my heart to hear. Just keep waiting I think God is telling me. Do not worry, Cecilia I have got this. I continue over the next several days to manage to stay in this faith filled valley. I know God is with me. He is walking beside me, holding my hand, and carrying me when I need him to. Thank you, Jesus! You dear reader, must do as it says in 1 Corinthians 11:13 and "Judge for yourselves."

It is a special blessing that I have not lost any bit of my faith, I know. It may be naïve to continue to hope after all this time that my husband will come back to me but Jesus raised Lazareth from the dead after four days, this could easily be done if it's God's will. Ecclesiastes 4:9 says "Two are better than one..." Verses 10-12 continue with "If one falls, the other will lift up his companion. Woe to the solitary man! For if he should fall, he has no one to lift him up. So also, if two sleep together, they keep each other warm. Where a lone man may be overcome, two can resist." This is what I am trying to do for my husband: lift him up in prayer and save our marriage. We may not have wholly had God at the forefront of our marriage, but we could change that and invite him in now and keep him there if we got a second chance!

12

❧

The Man from Missouri

How a mere 24 hours can change so much in my mind, I do not know but I decided on February twenty-seventh to plan a trip to Missouri to meet a new guy I'd been talking to online. Yesterday I was so focused on saving our marriage and waiting for my husband to return. Now I am planning a trip for the weekend to take a chance and meet someone new. Looking back, I wonder if it was the evil one attacking my faith and making me act rashly? In my journal I even wrote a note with the address to the hotel I would be staying at just in case someone needed to come looking for me. That shows my trepidation right there! I know I had no intentions of breaking my marriage vows, I wrote in my journal that even though my husband may be a cheater I would not be!

I know I was lonely at this point and feeling like I needed validation of my worth, especially from a man's point of view. I felt that my husband had abandoned me, and it had already been six long months since he announced his intentions. Despite the support from my family, I was feeling very alone. I turned to the bible for my nightly reading. Instead of the usual support, I found this line from 1 Samuel 4:17, "...And the ark of God has been captured." This made me feel nervous. Was I about to make a mistake? I resolved to remember that I was still married.

The next night I dreamt of my husband cheating on me with yet another woman. In my dream I decided to go find someone else too. This dream provided a rash of new thinking for me. Was I going to Missouri to meet someone because I had given up hope on my marriage or because I was hurt and wanted to feel better? In these moments, I knew I was not ready to give my heart to someone else, but a trip to another state felt like an adventure. A scary one, in a way, but maybe it was time to rip off the band-aid! As long as I don't break my marriage vows, I'll be fine, I rationalized. I prayed that God would guide me through this trial…

Matthew 12:14-15 "But the Pharisees went out and took counsel against him to put him to death. When Jesus realized this, he withdrew from that place." Uh-oh… That cannot be good, I think as I read this.

Being headstrong as I am, I forged ahead to Missouri anyway, despite the apparent warnings from the Holy Spirit. I had decided I could be faithful to my vows while investigating my future. If my husband did not want me, I could find someone that would. And I did. The man I met in Missouri was kind and honest right from the initial meeting. He showed me his driver's license and told me his history of where he came from and how he ended up in Missouri. At first, I thought it was too much information too soon, but I realized it was all information that could be easily verified and he was giving me reasons to trust who he was.

Being the nervous first-time dater that I was, I had a few drinks that night to make me less nervous. The Missouri man and I kissed that night. Looking back, I know I shouldn't have, but in the moment and considering my hurting heart it's easy to understand why it happened. However, I was very cognizant of not wanting to play the harlot and I went back to my hotel room alone. Opening my bible that night the messages from 2 Kings 17: 2-11 seemed even more straight forward and obviously meant to wake me up to stop my path "He did evil in the sight of the Lord… This came about because the Israelites sinned against the Lord… They adopted unlawful practices toward the Lord, their God… They did evil things that provoked the Lord… The Lord had told them, "You must not do this."

Hindsight is twenty-twenty, they say. I cannot remember if I read these words back then and thought they weren't for me, maybe they were for my husband. But it is as clear as crystal when I read them now that the Holy Spirit was speaking to me very loudly and very plainly that I must not do the things that I was doing! Even though that night I only kissed my date, the Holy Spirit was trying to tell me very plainly to not go down the road any further!

I truly hesitated to even include these sections in this story because it makes me feel so guilty that I clearly ignored God and his warnings. The whole time I was going through these trials brought on by my husband I felt like I was the victim. Here in these pages it is clear that even though I was still begging and praying to God for the miracle of saving my husband and my family, I was once again trying to take my life into my own hands and not willing to wait for God's plan to unfold. It literally hurts me to keep writing these words and admit my faults here, but I feel like these pages have to be included because in this world today it is so easy and so tempting for all of us going through the trials of separation or divorce to just give up and move on. That is not what we promised when we stood on the altar of God and said, "Until death do us part."

The next day, the man from Missouri reaches out to me as I drive home and says he would like to see me again. I smile to myself but then in the next second I stop because I wonder if I see him again will I be able to be so chaste the second or third or fourth time? Will I be able to live a chaste life for the rest of my life? I do not think so, I think to myself. I am just being honest here; I think my true trials have not even started yet. My marriage must be annulled before I can ever have relations with another man for it not to be considered adultery in the eyes of the Church. Not to mention just a few days ago I was crying my eyes out over my husband! I offer a silent plea: Lead me Lord!

That night the Holy Spirit sent me a friendlier message from Psalm 97:12. "Rejoice in the Lord, you just, and praise his holy name."

Back home in Illinois, daily, I ponder the situation with the man from Missouri and my pending divorce from my husband. Is this just a diversion? I know my heart still aches for my husband. The bible tells me in Deuteronomy 33:29 "...The Lord is your saving shield and his sword is your glory. Your enemies fawn upon you as you stride upon their heights." I realize I have not been down on my knees in prayer before bed in a long time. I think this is because it is in those moments that I truly confront my heart and I always end up crying when the truth comes out.

Tonight, I got down on my knees again and sure enough, the tears flowed like a leaky sieve. To be honest, I have been trying my best to ignore my heart! I pretend otherwise, but I know I am not over my husband. I do not think I ever will be-- I love him! I try to harden my thoughts for him daily and I thought I was doing a good job, but I know in the depths of my heart where the truth resides, that is a lie. I am not made that way. When I love, I love 100 percent. Last night I even dreamt we were getting back together. I know that is what my truest desires are. The real question is: What is God's plan?

I know it is not my place to question God or his plan. But I am so afraid I am going to mess it up! I want to be happy. But there has been no movement from my husband towards any sort of reconciliation and when I talk to the man from Missouri I do not have to think about my unhappy, non-existent marriage. I do not have to think about the hurt my husband has caused in these moments... Of course, at night my bible brings the truth back to me in Lamentations 5:11 "The wives of Zion were ravished by the enemy..." Not willing to go to sleep on that note, I read on in verses 15 "The joy of our heart has ceased..." and in verses 20-21 "Why then should you forget us, abandon us so long a time? Lead us back to you, O Lord, that we may be restored: Give us anew such days as we had of old."

Boy, do not ever let anyone tell you God does not know what is in your heart! Those lines are like a real conversation between me and God right there! It is like I am saying to God: man #2 gets my mind off the situation, God says, "No, it's not a good idea." I say: My heart hurts, that I feel like God is not with me. That I want the old days back like my marriage. I could not pick these lines out of the bible if I looked for them for days. Yet here God is telling me he knows what I was thinking in these moments!

However, in true fashion to my own nature, I fall back on my practices of old and begin to ignore God's warnings. I make plans to meet up with the man from Missouri. We schedule another date for St. Patrick's Day. I rationalize that we can schedule ourselves into mass; I can test him to see if he really is Catholic like he says. The bible readings I find tell me in Job 3:25-26 "For what I fear overtakes me, and what I shrink from comes upon me. I have no peace nor ease; I have no rest, for trouble comes!" In my deep inner-mind I think this cannot be a good sign; I even write the words "uh-oh..." in my journal. But I do not take any heed to them and I forge on ahead, once again thinking my ways are better than God's ways.

Over the course of the next several days my emotions run the gamut of high and low. One moment I am excited in the prospect of potential in the man from Missouri, the next I'm heartbroken all over again when my husband fails, yet again, to respond to a text message or phone call from me. My mother in law even calls to talk to me about the heartache she is experiencing over this divorce. I, of course, have no words for her because I am a swinging pendulum of indecision in these days.

One of my protestant friends tells me in detail how it is good for me to be talking to this man from Missouri. She explains that I am no longer bound to my marriage vows because the husband is the head of the household and he has already broken the marriage pact between us when he stepped out first. She explains that the husband is to be the leader of the house in all things, including the responsibility of making the marriage work and when he gave up on it, I was released from my bond. Unsure if this is actually accurate or not, I decide to go with it because it certainly makes me feel better in my current situation.

I also hear from my attorney that the divorce is proceeding at an expected pace, no thanks to my husband's attorney. Apparently, my husband's lawyer is trying to convince him to sue me for half of everything, including my retirement! Thank goodness my lawyer decides to file paperwork earlier and try to speed things up, so I do not end up penniless as well as heartbroken in the midst of this terrible process. Despite the broils of anger approaching, the main feeling I notice within me is that of being numb. I never wanted any of this and I was resolved to not allow him to take anything else from me: He already had my pride, my heart, and my feelings of self-worth. He could not have another thing! I had to hold on and trust in God's plan for me.

13

The Truth Hurts

March thirnteeth was one of the worst days on record. My husband had called me on my way to work and offered to come over and fix the window and kitchen drawer. In exchange he wanted to pick up his weight equipment and his tools. However, he did not want me to be home when he was there. I flat out said no. He seemed surprised and asked me why? I told him I would not let any other stranger in my house to do repairs without supervision. Boy, oh boy, did he get mad about that! Oh well, I guess. This was not just about him anymore.

This upset me so much, despite my bravado on the phone, I was unable to compose myself enough to walk into work in my normal "fake it 'til I make it" way. The ladies in the office immediately knew something was very wrong when I made a beeline straight into my office and shut the door behind me. I stayed there alone for twenty minutes, but to no avail. I could not get myself together; my emotions had finally taken over, regardless of the fact that I was in my safety net: work. Finally, I called my secretary and asked her to assemble the crew of my closest, most trusted colleagues. Within minutes, the five of them were assembled in the conference room and I was confessing the secret that I had been living with for the past seven months: my husband had left me, I was alone, and on the brink of divorce.

They were shocked, sad, even heartbroken for me; I believe. Susan even started crying. Seeing their faces and their genuine concern and compassion for me I broke down even further. I was allowing them to see me at my core: battered and bruised-- the exact opposite of the professional image I tried so hard to project every day in my school. My breathing started to hitch, and my words became jumbled, lost in the emotion and heartache of the truth breaking free.

After this revelation occurred, I left the office and went home for the rest of the day. Proverbs 25:2 comforted me that afternoon with its words "God has glory in what he conceals, kings have glory in what they fathom. As the heavens in height, and the earth in depth, the heart of kings is unfathomable." Lord knows how this plan would all work out, but He was keeping it a secret from me for now.

The hidden beauty at this point in the story is the fact that so many of my friends and relatives had begun praying for me, for us, for our marriage, and for our whole family. It was not just a battle between my husband and I; our families on both sides of the isle were hurting too. Of course, his parents had been upfront with me and him about how they wanted us to work things out, even going so far as to try and arrange "family meetings" in attempts to get us in the same room together. I fell for that at Christmas, but the outcome was so horrible: him ignoring me and most of his family at that dinner, that I decided I would not put them through that again.

My mother was heartbroken. Not just to see me in tears at every meeting, but because she absolutely loved and respected my husband so much. She kept thinking that if his mind could just be cleared, if he would just pray or think about what was in the best interest of everyone involved he would come back to me and to the person he used to be. Once, before he actually moved out of the house, I had told him I would wait for him, no matter how long it took for the real him to come back. I shared with my mother his words that haunt me still to this day "Do you know how long that could take me? To get back to how I used to be?"

But in my mind and my mother's mind those words made us think that maybe there was a chance...

Another time, during a verbal argument, I told my husband I wanted to talk to my REAL husband, not this new person I did not know. He actually answered me in the third person, saying "He hasn't been around for a long time." Those words made the prayer fires start up again in our whole families anew. Three of my uncles, two aunts, and a great-aunt that was a nun were all praying trying to save us. Of course, there was the chance that "it had been too long. He would've come back by now if he was coming back." When Sister Mary Louise told my mother that, it was like another nail in the coffin being hammered. I thought if she believed it was too late, and she was a woman of God, then what hope could I have?

I spent the next three weekends in Missouri. We went to dinners, clubs, movies. We spent time with his friends. We talked about likes and dislikes, how we believe relationships should work, and how neither of us wanted to see anyone else in the dating world. Everything I can learn about him tells me he is an honest, sincere man. We laugh and joke and talk! Oh, how I have missed talking to a man. I invited him to come to Illinois and be my date for my sister's wedding in October. It is only March now, but all signs are pointing to the good!

One of the "signs" I consider is the fact that both Catholic churches that flank the place where my Missouri man lives are named after two very important saints that I have been specifically praying with along this journey. St. Monica's Church and St. Joseph's Church. For the first time in several weeks I consult with my bible and find Job chapters 30-31. "... Let thorns grow instead of wheat, and foul weeds instead of barley..." It seems to me that the days of me finding comfort in God's words are over. Why am I finding these painful verses? I did not ask for this divorce but now I feel like it is me doing something wrong. If I am honest, I can say for sure the Holy Spirit is still trying to influence me, reach for me, giving me signs of warning every time I open the Good Book.

However, it seems that my only escape from heartbreak is in Missouri. April finds me on a Friday evening waiting for my "husband" to come by and pick up the rest of his things. We have agreed that he can have his weight equipment, his four-wheeler ATV, and half of our pictures. I set the pictures on the kitchen counter, still in their binders, piles, picture frames, and wedding albums. I had to take them all off the shelves and walls months ago and they are still how I left them.

He begins to thumb through a picture album of the two of us and our adventures together. He shuts it before getting halfway through. He picks up our wedding album and flips through three pages and stops, shutting the cover. I look up from my place in the living room (I had wanted to give the impression that I was giving him privacy but was secretly stealing glances every chance I got.) He announced that he changed his mind and that I could have all the pictures.

"What am I going to do with them all?" I ask incredulously. I noticed his face was red and he looked extremely uncomfortable. I pushed even further. "At least take the ones with you and your groomsmen from our wedding. I mean they're still your friends!" I begin pulling them out of their sleeves. "And here, take this album. It has all the pictures of the work you have done remodeling our two houses. You could use these when you start your business of flipping homes." He had wanted to do that for a while, and when I brought that up, it caused him to jerk just a little in response. He stammered ok, but that was all he would take. He took a little longer glance at our honeymoon picture from Senor Frog's in Mexico, then cleared his throat and backed away from the kitchen altogether. There was emotion in that man, I could see it! He was choking it back, but I saw it and I took a chance...

On the steps between the office and the garage, as he was trying to run away from our life yet again, I grabbed his hand and stopped him. Choking back tears of my own, I held his hand and looked up into his aqua-green eyes. With all my heart I told him, "I never wanted any of this to happen. I am so sorry for everything that I did."

The dark cloud seemed to lift from his face, and I felt like he was actually seeing me and hearing my words. I felt him squeeze my hand, just a little— and our eyes locked onto each other like they were in silent communication with each other, like they used to do. Neither of us said a word, nor breathed from what I could tell. Then suddenly he pulled his hand back from mine and walked down the steps towards his truck, away from me and away from the life we had built together.

I stood at the top of the steps, frozen, yet silent tears were still able to flow down my cheeks. This was the worst hurt anyone could possibly ask another person to endure! Watching the love of my life walk away and being powerless to stop it.

It was mid-April when I stumbled across yet another revelation. For the first time since this heartbreak marathon had begun, I realized I would have to sell my house and our boat. Especially the boat, I think. I cannot enjoy it without my husband. Yes, I can drive it, but I will not enjoy it without him! If we are not together, then these things mean nothing to me. They simply represent my loss and hurt. I do not need that in my life. I want to be happy!

By the end of the month, my home refinance paperwork is in order and I have a buyer for the boat. My husband finds out I am selling the boat and tries to get me to sell it to him for what we owe on it. Out of spite, I refuse; telling him to let his new woman buy him a new boat! It was childish, I know, but he had signed the separation agreement and I was not feeling too charitable as I still felt like this was all his fault! The divorce date has been set. Eight months earlier my husband had told me "we were on our way out." I guess now it is official.

If there was ever a car that traveled more slowly to the courthouse than mine did on that divorce day, you could have fooled me. I did not want to go, and my engine knew it. I trudged up the court steps and through the security checkpoints in a daze. I started crying when my lawyer and I were still in the clerk's office signing some preliminary paperwork. When we walked out of that door, my husband was sitting on the bench outside in the hall. I stared at him, willing him to look at me. My brain was screaming: There's still time to stop this! He did not move, didn't look up.

My lawyer guided me probably, but it felt like being herded, into the court room. My table and my husband's table were set facing each other, yet angled slightly to the judges large, oversized "bench." I was shaking, literally—shaking from my nerves, anxiety, depression, anger, hurt— everything. My husband walked into the courtroom, shoulders back, jaw set, lips tight.

Whatever the words were for the next moments are still a blur to me; I have no recollection of what exactly was said. What I do remember is that my husband would not look at me. Not once during the entire proceeding did he glance in my direction or even acknowledge that I was in the room. I watched him the entire time. He managed to look at the judge, his lawyer, my lawyer—everyone but me.

As I signed the divorce paperwork the judge tried to impart some words of wisdom or consolation. I think it was because I cried during the ENTIRE process. He said, "This may not be what you wanted, but in the end it's better to part ways then wake up next to a stranger. When the person you're with is not the person you know anymore."

I ran away from the courthouse in the exact opposite fashion in which I arrived-- as fast as my legs and my car could carry me. I drove straight to Nina's Bar; no one I knew would be there. It was only ten o'clock in the morning, but I had never needed a shot of tequila more than I needed it then. As I sat there, smoking, and drinking alone knowing full well I was the complete cliché of a divorced woman in that moment it finally hit me: IT IS FINALLY FINISHED.

Except that it was not. Finished that is. It was not finished for me, not by a long shot. I learned later that week that my husband drove to the golf course to meet his brother after our divorce papers were signed. At first, I was outraged. Here I was, drinking alone in a bar completely destroyed and he went out for a round of golf? But my brother-in-law confided to me that my husband actually broke down sobbing on the green, unable to be consoled even by his brother. To this day, the image of this scene haunts me.

PART

TWO

14

God Makes Me Slow Down

I can remember the exact date and moment in time that my life as I knew it started to fall apart. Our lost adoption and my father-in-law's heart attack also happened on that day. My husband fell into a deep depression which spiraled into his reaching out to another woman for support and comfort. I, though remaining strong in my faith and gaining a personal relationship with Jesus, had begun to drink my dinners on an almost nightly basis and avoided being inside "our" home as much as I possibly could. Our pictures were down, the furniture was rearranged, and I was going through the motions trying to start over.

Exactly one year later I was trying to start over. The man from Missouri and I were flying to South America to visit his family for a week. He had not been home in years and I needed a change in scenery. To be honest, I was having feelings for this man, despite my deep love for my now (by Illinois law) ex-husband, and maybe meeting this new family would help ease some of the wounds I felt from having to forcibly give up the family of my husband. I found myself cautiously optimistic about the prospects of this trip. At the root of everything, I trusted in God's overall plan for my life and hoped that perhaps this was part of it.

On our final night in Sao Paulo, Brazil, his family threw us a going away party at his oldest brother's home. This event involved the entire immediate family: his four brothers, his sister, three nieces, two nephews, their wives, girlfriends, or husbands, and his mother. There was a fancy dinner on real china plates, wine, flowers on the table, everyone dressed up, there was a DJ playing dance music, and I even learned how to salsa that night! At one point in the evening I stood back in the corner, apart from the group, surveying the scene of laughter, fun, and love. Before I knew what was happening, I discovered tears were welling over and spilling down onto my cheeks. I turned my face quickly to wipe them away, but my man from Missouri was very attentive to me and noticed, asking, "Que pasa?" I explained that his family was so wonderful and loving. It was truly touching my heart to see it and to be a part of it in this moment. In my soul, I was thanking God for allowing me to witness this love and to realize that there is another family that would find me worthy to so readily accept me and allow me know that love is still alive in the world despite my own personal heartbreak. I was overcome with this knowledge and that was why I was crying. God was continuing to be good to me, despite my weaknesses.

Fast forward to August 2013. It was one month after my trip to South America, four days away from my 40th birthday. I was feeling beautiful, skinny, strong from working out regularly, in control, and as close to loving life as my divorced self could! It felt like it had taken me a while to get to this place, but it felt really good to be there! That night I was meeting my best friend out for dinner and drinks to "celebrate" my birthday. We have been friends since high school and since it is a weeknight, we decided to keep it low-key. We were meeting at some new po-dunk place that just opened in between where we both live in the "country." Just dinner and a couple drinks, maybe. Nothing crazy on our agenda for the night. We both had to work the next day!

September fourteenth: actual journal entry; *"It's been a long time since I wrote in this journal. I've been dating Christian since the Spring. We went to Brazil together in July. I thought I was getting myself together. Four days before my birthday, I met Michelle out for dinner at "The Backwoods" in Maytown. I ate dinner and had two beers. I started to feel queasy to my stomach and thought I better sit down. Soon, I felt ok, so I went out to look at a former student's motorcycle. Next thing I know I'm in the back of an emergency squad being taken to the hospital. They said I fainted, fell back, and hit my head on concrete. They said I tried to sit up and reached for my head and fell back again, hitting my head again. They said I was unconscious, stopped breathing, my lips turned blue, then I gasped for breath. A few days later, I went to the neurologist for an MRI appointment after the initial CAT scan at the ER. They rushed me back to the emergency room again. My brain was bleeding. I had four bleeds: one large, 50 cent piece-sized on the frontal lobe, one on each temporal lobe, and one on the back of my brain where it initially hit the concrete. As of now, I've been off work for three and a half weeks. This is the first day I've been able to focus enough to see straight and hold a pen to write. My other symptoms include a numb, tingly lower lip, strong headaches, major dizziness, loss of balance and coordination, inability to concentrate, eye twitches, major instant mood swings, depression, sleepiness, fatigue, and I can't smell or taste anything. I'm on anti-seizure medication and anti-dizziness medicine. I'm not allowed to drive, exercise, or go back to work for at least another four weeks, depends on my next doctor's visit. They're sending me to the Brain and Trauma Center for further testing or rehab. My family is fearful that they could've lost me. I'm also on a 30-day heart monitor to see if I have an irregular heartbeat that could've caused the fainting episode. They are pretty sure I didn't have a seizure but are keeping me on the meds, just in case. My dad and my best friend think someone spiked my beer with something illegal, but IDK.*

I went to confession today. I am trying to let everything go and let God. That's what my Grandma Elaine always used to say: Let Go Let God. I obviously am not in control. My mom said when God wants to draw you closer to him, he uses things like this to do it. Right now, I feel empty. I've already lost my husband and any potential for a family of my own, now my ability to exercise (health), also my ability to work, which is my first love and my sense of pride. I'm starting to feel a bit like Job from the Bible-- totally stripped and beat down.

So, I've decided to try and relax. What other choice do I have? I'm inviting God back into my life fully, today. What am I supposed to learn? Here I am. My plans were obviously not his plans. Dear God, please comfort me and guide me. Teach me to put you first before all things. Help me trust in you and allow your will to take over."

The following bible verses are written in my journal on this day, as was my practice. *Matthew 10:22 "You will be hated by all because of my name, but whoever endures to the end will be saved."*

Matthew 10:26-33 "...Therefore do not be afraid of them. Nothing is concealed that will not be revealed, nor secret that will not be known."

For the first time in a long time, I write the words that have been in my heart for a while. These thoughts come to my mind as if spoken to me by the Holy Spirit himself: Write this book. Go speak to conventions about your struggles with divorce.

Today I had a rough emotional morning. For no reason really. It is just that I realized that tomorrow is my ex-husband's birthday. I know he does not deserve my thoughts, yet I continue to think about him, even still think of him as my husband. I broke down and mailed him a birthday card. I felt like I had to. I wrote in the card that I wished him well and I was trying to forgive and forget and to also let go of his family. I know he really wants me to do that. He feels like I stole their loyalties and he wants that back.

I wrote that I hoped he could learn to not resent me (for whatever reason he has). I wrote to him that for some reason I could not close the door on our relationship and that I hoped that someday we'd be able to talk like we used to do. I felt like I needed to do that for some reason, but I do not know why I felt that way. He did not even acknowledge me or my accident or my subsequent health problems. He has not said a word to my sister—who he works with every day. He hasn't asked his parents about me, even though they came to visit me at the hospital, and he knows they did through his brother. Why am I bothering to send this card? He probably will not even read it, much less open it! If he does, he probably will not understand what I'm trying to say. What I do know is that I still love him. Writing and mailing that card was peace for me. I think it was a way for me to put it in God's hands. From here, I will never know the path of that card from the moment I place it in the mailbox. Only God will know and that is enough for me right now.

Dear God, please bring us all peace and comfort in this journey. I do not know why we are on this path or what the outcome will be. Jesus, I trust in you.

From my Bible readings tonight, I think a little bit of clarity comes through to me. I think my husband is struggling in the darkness. Even though he was baptized and became Catholic, he does not have the strength and knowledge, the strong belief to stay the course when he met a trying time. In Wisdom 19:16-17 I read, "Yet these, after welcoming them with festivities, oppressed with awful toils those who now shared with them the same rights. And they were struck with blindness, as those others had been at the portals of the just—When, surrounded by yawning darkness, each sought the entrance of his own gate."

I must continue to pray for my husband. Even though it is hard. It is extremely painful to even think of him. I must for myself and for him continue to trust in God and in his plan for goodness.

My doctor said because of this head injury I could expect my emotions to swing wildly at times. He said I may be happy one moment and then swing almost crazily into tears or frustration or anger almost instantly. Couple that with my emotions of still going through the sting of divorce and I am a mess. I think since I cannot drive or work, being stuck at home, I have little to do but ruminate on what my brain last remembers: a horrific tragedy that broke my heart. Up until the point of this standstill— where I cannot do ANYTHING—I was wonderfully, blissfully, perfectly ignoring the pain in my heart. I had swum through the outpouring of my tears and built a dam around my heart where I was able to safely live at the top of my tower pretending, I had a new prince. This new prince lived in Missouri, so he was a safe distance away and I could escape to his far away land whenever I needed to have an adventure. He was exciting and loving, and I could keep him at an arm's length until I wanted a change.

Being stuck at home with a brain injury that I could not control was torture in a new way. I had previously been pouring a large amount of energy into my job and now that had been yanked away from me. Now I was able to get updates on my "husband." Updates that I both desperately craved and cringed at getting simultaneously. I could not help myself. I was like a child being told not to touch a hot stove. Was it really as hot as they said? Oh yes, it was!

The day came for my "ex-husband's" birthday. There, I said it. Ex-husband. By the state of Illinois, he was an ex. Maybe it's God's plan for him to be the stepfather to HER kids. He took the boy to play paintball for my ex's birthday this weekend. I found out through his parents. They went there to bring him his traditional birthday apple pie and saw them together. Of course, then SHE came around the corner and they got to meet HER too. How fun. (Insert sarcasm.)

He told his parents that he is realizing there "are bigger things in the world than just himself." Oh, how that stings my heart! We could have had a family! I do not understand why God does not want to bless me with a family! I am trying hard to let go and let God, but this is like a knife to my heart! I mean, really? Meanwhile, I am stuck in no man's land with a head injury!

I know my mom said maybe God is trying to draw me nearer to him, but good grief! Why do I always have to suffer? I am a good person!... I know I am being selfish and untrusting even as I write this entry... but I'm so tired of hurting!!!!!

Dear God, please allow me to feel peace and love and comfort. Maybe I do not truly deserve it, but I try.

15

Anger Wrapped Up in Prayer

Tonight in Sirach 25:1 it is said to me: With three things I am delighted, for they are pleasing to the Lord and to men: Harmony among brethren, friendship among neighbors, and the mutual love of husband and wife. Sirach 25:8 tells me: Happy is he who dwells with a sensible wife, and he who plows not like a donkey yoked with an ox."

Sirach always brings me peace as I feel it speaks wisdom to me. This reading clues me into two thoughts: 1) A husband and wife must have mutual love to make God happy. I do believe that my husband and I had mutual love between us. However, was that love lasting in a mutual way? I can only speak for myself, honestly. Maybe God is telling me something here. I realize this is a repeat reading for me. The word mutual stands out to me again. It is the important word to focus on, as if the love is not mutual it is not real. 2) I do not think my husband will be happy with HER. 'Like a donkey yoked to an ox'—that's symbolism for a struggle right there. (But maybe that is not a nice, Christian thought for me to have.)

I just must renew my patience. I know better than to pray for patience because when you do, God gives you opportunities to practice patience! I do not want to practice it anymore. I just want to BE patient. I also know that when I am not trusting in God's plan I am being like Peter when he looks away from Jesus on the stormy waters when he was walking across the sea. Or even more like when Peter denied Jesus three times before the cocked crowed on the night they came to take Jesus away to be crucified. I do not want to be like Peter in that instance! I would rather be like Peter when he went forth and spread the good news of Jesus and traveled around telling everyone of the wonderful miracles.

I am 40 years old now. If I do not have patience by now, is it possible to learn it? *Dear God, please help me be patient in waiting for your wonderful plan for me to unfold.*

The next night, I meet with my personal trainer. Not to work-out, I am not cleared for any of that. She just comes over to talk. Occasionally, we meet to have a heart to heart. I guess it was time for one of those, given my medical condition. Right now, there are many hypotheses about what caused me to faint and hit my head. She thinks I fainted from stress and now after all this time my body is forcing me to take a break and deal with everything. I tell her I do not want to do that.

She thinks I have been in denial about my feelings. Of course, I agree. I've always hoped that if I pushed hard enough and for long enough, I would just get over it. Meaning get over everything. So now, she says, I must take this forced time out and deal with it all and accept it and allow myself to grieve. I have to give up my mother-in-law, my father-in-law, my brother and sister-in-law; even give up the family dog we gave them, and I truly love Rosie. We rescued her together...

She is right, of course. My "ex-husband" has had plenty of time and plenty of chances to do the right thing. For whatever reason he has not. He just has not. End of story.

Dear God, please help me cope, accept, and move on according to your will. I lost my husband and that is not what I wanted. I do have faith in you and your plan. Please fill me with peace. This same night I open my bible to 1 Maccabees 3:19-22 and read some very striking and inspiring words. This process is so meaningful to me! God's words to me "For victory in war does not depend upon the size of the army, but on the strength that comes from

Heaven. With great presumption and lawlessness, they come against us to destroy us and our wives and children and to despoil us; but we are fighting for our lives and our laws. He himself will crush them before us; so, do not be afraid of them."

Wow. Just wow! God is telling me to not be afraid. What I have known all along, since the beginning of this struggle—since the moment my husband said he wasn't happy—was that this was a war I had to fight. God himself is telling me he is with me and will help me crush the enemy. Come what may, I must remain strong, focused, and faithful.

I am beginning to learn that my emotions are going to come in waves now. There will be patches of roughness and periods of smoother road. Today was rougher than yesterday in moments. I can feel my anger and frustration. Maybe this is because I am trying to allow myself to BE angry. Don't I have a right to be mad? Anger is a natural emotion. It will help me heal to acknowledge that. If I do not allow the anger to fester or lash out at people, then the anger itself is okay. I am also trying to convince myself that my marriage and my head injury "is what it is" and my life is not over. What I thought were my happiest moments surely were not. God must have something bigger and better in store for me. I know he wants me to be happy!

Dear God, please help me to accept and process this loss quickly and to the best of my ability. Please bless my efforts according to your will. Amen.

I feel like tonight's reading in the bible gives me an immediate response from Daniel 3:47. He says, "Truly your God is the God of gods and Lord of Kings and a revealer of mysteries; that is why you were able to reveal this mystery."

Is there a bigger word in the dictionary than WOW? I feel that I am having a very personal and direct conversation with God here and throughout this journal. Thank you, God. This is amazing! I do not know what it all means, I just believe that you are talking with me and helping me here.

My parents have decided to take a trip to Florida. Why not? They are retired, they can enjoy the life and do what they want, whenever the mood strikes them. They have invited me to go with them. It is nearing the end of September by this point; I've been off work for about four weeks and the doctor is not releasing me to go back anytime soon. In fact, my best friend is still spending the night with me most nights, keeping an eye on me to make sure I do not fall and hit my head again. More than being a safety precaution though, I suspect she feels guilty about what happened to me the night I fainted and hit my head. She had stepped away to take a phone call and when she looked over, I was collapsed on the ground. I think she was trying to make it up to me (or herself) and trying to take care of me now.

I had a choice to make about whether to travel with my parents to Florida for a week. On one hand, I felt guilty at the thought at taking what sounded like a vacation when in any other season I would be firmly positioned at the helm of running an elementary school. On the other hand, I had suffered a life-threatening injury and was unable to work, exercise, or drive. I could not even take myself to the grocery store, which was four miles away, without assistance from someone! Even with a brain injury I was able to see the sense in going with my parents on a vacation!

There were periods of time on any given day when I would begin to have better emotional experiences. I enjoyed getting a manicure and pediure this morning and going to see a movie with a friend today. Later I helped her adopt a dog. Maybe most importantly on that day, when I returned home, I did not cry. I was able to take that as a good sign. I started to look forward to the trip with my parents to Florida. The thought came to mind that I not only needed to emotionally distance myself from the events of the last several months, but perhaps a physical distance from this space and history would help me too.

Tonight, I pray to God that he will continue to bless me and my family with renewed healing and patient faith. I find in the bible the chapter from Numbers 30:10-16. *"And if she vowed in her husband's house, or bound herself by a pledge with an oath, and her husband heard of it, and said nothing to her, and did not oppose her; then all her vows shall stand, and every pledge by which she bound herself shall stand. But if her husband makes them null and void on the day that he hears of them, then whatever proceeds out of her lips concerning her vows, or concerning her pledge of herself, shall not stand: her husband has made them void, and the LORD will forgive her. Any vow and any binding oath to afflict herself, her husband may establish, or her husband may make void. But if her husband says nothing to her from day to day, then he establishes all her vows, or all her pledges, that are upon her; he has established them, because he has said nothing to her on the day that he heard of them. But if he makes them null and void after he has heard of them, then he shall bear her iniquity. These are the statutes which the LORD commanded Moses, as between a man and his wife..."*

To this day I struggle with this reading. Did my husband nullify my vows or not? He was terribly angry when he learned that I was dating someone else. So much so that we erupted into a huge fight over the phone with my ex calling the man from Missouri every racial slur in the book, names I had never heard him say towards anyone. Events like that made me think my husband was not so sure he wanted to let me go, divorce or not. Other times I heard nothing from him; he had no voice at all during the divorce hearing, he only responded with one line on the annulment paperwork: give her whatever she wants. If it were his husbandly duty to free me or hold me bound to my vows I couldn't and still cannot discern which he had done.

My father-in-law was taken by emergency squad to Memorial Hospital just days before I am scheduled to leave for Florida with my parents. In normal fashion, my first response was to rush right there as fast as I could. But I could not drive!! God bless my sister. She drove 30 minutes to get me and then another 30 to the hospital. When we arrived at 9 p.m. my mother-in-law was crying because my "ex-husband" was not there. What?! Surely, he would come to the hospital when we did not know what was wrong with his dad? They were thinking it was his heart again. Just a little over a year ago he had survived the widow maker surgery and here he was in the hospital again. It was the duty of the oldest son to come and at least comfort his mother, right?

All I could think was that there was something so obviously broken in the man that had been my husband. I thought he must be so fearful and scarred from what he experienced the last time his dad went by life-flight chopper to Memorial Hospital. I wondered if my ex-husband couldn't steel himself yet again to square up against this fortress of a hospital. In my mind's eye, I can imagine his strong, wide shoulders set, his jaw tight, fists clenched with his mom hanging onto him for dear-life as they walked his father out to the helicopter on the roof top last year. I could almost understand how he could not come to see his father this time around until 10am the next day, almost 24 hours later. By that time, they had all but ruled out heart and were thinking more towards an infection. I could assume he felt less stress by that point.

It hurt my heart to know the man I love (or loved?) was in so much pain and unable to handle his stress. However, I do feel some little sort of relief to realize that he is human and not some sort of evil monster I was beginning to believe. Not that it changes our situation, of course. Not that it takes away any of the hurt he has caused me. It makes me want to want to not hate him. I never wanted to hate him. I do not hate him. I cannot even type that he is not my husband, of course I don't hate him... I am angry. Of course, I am angry. I have a right to be angry with him. We made promises to each other. There is so much love in my heart... still... but it is wrapped up in confusion and anger and guilt...

Despite all of that, it does make me want to forgive him more. How do I do that?

All this stress is not good for my own health. I have felt dizzy again and more emotional in the past few days. I must let my old life go and I must have the strength to let the family go. My ex-husband is not moving towards me and I have no control over that. My life is truly in God's hands and it is taken a brain injury to make me realize it. I cannot even work until he heals my brain, literally. I just pray that he heals my heart soon too.

Dear God, please watch over the family and heal my father-in-law. Please allow my faith to positively influence them. Every time I think to plan on releasing them from my heart, something happens to pull me back. Please allow both our families to be blessed with peace, love, and health. Please also watch over my older sister's father-in-law during and after his surgery this week. It feels like our family is under attack; I know this year we are concentrating our prayers for the family. I know the evil one attacks the family as an attempt to break down both our faith and our society. Please allow my prayers to cover us as a blanket and wrap us in your love. 9/23/13.

That night the Holy Spirit answers my prayers through Ezekiel 8:10. "See, the day of the Lord! See, the end is coming! Lawlessness is in full bloom, insolence flourishes, violence has risen to support wickedness. It shall not be long in coming, nor shall it delay. The time has come, the day dawns. Let not the buyer rejoice nor the seller mourn, for wrath shall be upon all the throng. The seller shall not regain what he sold as long as he lives, for wrath shall be upon all the throng. Because of his sins, no one shall preserve his life. They shall sound the trumpet and make everything ready, yet no one shall go to war, for my wrath is upon all the throng."

This answer sends me back into prayer. I ask God: *Please God, spare the family from any more stress, illness, and despair. Please heal them and show them your divine mercy and love. If it be your will. Amen.*

16

Tears That Heal

The next day, over coffee with one of my best friends, I am asked a most pointed question. Is the man I am dating the love of my life? My answer is sad, but true. I believe that my husband was the love of my life. I truly, honestly believe that he was. I think that he is. I mean, he is still alive. At least the man I married was the love of my life. Or should I say, the man I dated and was married to for a combined 10 years was the love of my life.

I am still so upset about everything! What if I never get over him? I know God has a plan. I just know it. I need to TRUST & BELIEVE...

Dear God, you know what I want in my heart. You know what is best for me. Will my annulment go through? Will my husband realize he made a mistake and try to correct it? Will I be happy again? How can I be so miserable if he is not the one?

Today, like a strong scolding to a child who is listening, the Holy Spirit answers me. This time my lesson comes from John 10:24. "So the Jews gathered around him and said to him, "How long are you going to keep us in suspense? If you are the Messiah, tell us plainly. Jesus answered them, "I told you and you did not believe..."

I feel like in this moment, God is telling me to look back on the previous day's reading. He has told me, "…because of his sins, no one shall preserve his life…" doesn't that mean my marriage is over? Even in the eyes of the church? My old life is over. Pick up the pieces, Cecilia, and move on. What other choice do I have?

Several days pass before I write in my journal again. I have decided to travel to Florida with my parents. I think the trip away will do good for me. It is a little bit like hiding out, but easier to cope with everything here, in a foreign place like Florida than it is at my own house. My father-in-law called to tell me he is out of the hospital. He thanks me for coming to see him and tells me that he loves me. Even as I write this, tears begin to trickle down my cheeks. They do every time I think of my father-in-law. Why am I so weak? When I try to deal with this, all I can do is cry. Maybe if I stop thinking about my sorrow, I can live my life. I do not think it will feel like moving on, but at least I won't be stuck in this place I know as "Tears Ville."

Today, while I was alone at the pool, in the middle of sunny Florida, I cried. The emotion overtook me so much that I found myself repeating the words: God loves me. God loves me. God loves me. Twelve times I repeated it until I could stop crying.

That night in my journal I wrote my prayer of thanks. *Dear God, thank you for allowing my father-in-law to get better and for my sister's father-in-law to have a good surgery. Please watch over and keep my family safe, healthy, and happy for as long as possible. When I read the bible tonight, what do you want me to know?*

God answered me again in Isaiah 18:3. "All you who inhabit the world, who dwell on earth, when the signal is raised on the mountain, look! When the trumpet blows, listen!" Obviously, to me, God is telling me to pay attention to the signs, the sights, and the sounds that are all around me. Really, this is a lesson for all of us, as I look back on this and begin to see a more global view of my journey. But in that moment, I am viewing the events of my life through a microscope and living day to day, scraping the surface of darkness, trying to stay afloat on the river to my new life and hopefully find happiness again.

The next morning, I awoke from a dream-filled night. I had silently cried myself to sleep, not wanting my parents to hear my anguish. I had burdened them so much already. In my dream, my husband had come to find me to talk. He found me at some party I was attending and told me he wanted me back. He had some small gifts for me and asked me to step away from my friends so we could talk in private. In my dream we did not talk about the time we'd been apart or what we'd been doing. Instead we talked about our feelings for each other and the love we still felt…

I must have had some kind of look on my face that morning because my dad came over to my side of the room, sat beside me and said I looked mad.

"What's wrong?" He then put his arms around me, and I said, "Yes! I am mad!"

"Why are you mad?" He asked me.

I could not allow myself to put it into words. I knew I would either erupt like a volcano with so much anger I did not know if I were able to reign it back in or I would collapse into a puddle of soggy tears. Instead I managed to eke out, "I'm mad because…because…. You know why I'm mad!"

He just gave me a big, huge, hug and said that he, for one, was so grateful for all the time we'd been able to spend together lately and how we wouldn't have had this time if certain things were different. Of course, he was right. And I agreed. I gave him a big hug and a kiss and thanked him for being here for me.

Of course, he did not even know how awfully close to the truth he really was: if CERTAIN things were different, we would not be having this mother-daughter-father vacation together. I mean, I had practically asked for this on the corner of Deally and Castle Roads… I am quite sure that conversation with my dad was my own personal trumpet blowing for me to pay attention to…

Some time ago, before my husband came home and told me how unhappy he was, my dad was sick. I do not know to the full extent exactly how sick he was, I just remember that there were prayers involved and most likely miracles too. I know before we even got married there was a scare as to whether he would be there to dance with me at my wedding and somehow, he pulled out of that. On this day I am remembering, I was just about home, about a quarter mile, stopped at the stop sign on the corner of Castle and Deally Road. In less than 30 seconds I would be pulling into our driveway, home from a day's work. Heavy on my mind in that moment was the possibility of losing my dad because of his health. I was scared. In my mind, out of nowhere, a question formed: Would you sacrifice your husband for your father? Feeling a prayer, I asked God to please save my dad and keep him here with us. If I must lose my husband to keep my father, I will. God help me, I love my husband. I do not know why I'm thinking this, but I would give up my husband to have my dad around for as long as you see fit.

I never thought of this moment in time again, until of course many tears into the break-up of my marriage. I know that like Abraham being willing to sacrifice his child for God the Father, I was willing to sacrifice my love, my husband, to save my dad. I do not think that God called me out on that offer, but I do know that my dad is still here with us and for that I am very grateful.

Thinking of that day long ago, I pray to God, thanking him for that extra time with my parents. I thank him for improving my father-in-law's health. I pray that my husband realizes how important time is with his family. He too, has been given the gift of time. I also pray that the man I loved still exists somewhere in that locked down heart. I pray for blessings for my two brothers and two sisters. I pray that all my extended family, my in-laws, their family, and the family of the man from Missouri are all watched over. Please God, help me heal. Help me grow patient and wise so I can see what your plan is for me and for my life.

That night in the bible, I am shown 2 Kings 2:1-10. "When the Lord was about to take Elijah up to heaven in a whirlwind he and Elisha were on their way from Gilgal. "Stay here please," Elijah said to Elisha… "As the Lord lives and you yourself live," Elisha replied, "I will not leave you." (9) "May I receive a double portion of your spirit." (10) "You have asked for something that is not easy," he replied. "Still if you see me taken up from you, your wish will be granted; otherwise not."

On September 28, 2013 I believe I received another strong message to write down the events of these past few months. It comes to me at the beginning of my journal writings: Write your book! I find in Jeremiah 30:2, "Thus says the Lord: Write in a book all the words that I have spoken to you." I know my journal has helped me heal. I hope what I have found can help others to heal as well.

This day was a better day emotionally for me than some others in this week have been. However, I did break down to my mother again. I confessed to her how weak I felt for still crying and not being over him. She told me she thought I was normal—better than normal. She told me to consider all the stress I had been through this year, and then pile on top of that my recent head injury and the fact that I was lucky to be alive. She reminded me although it was almost a year since he had moved out, the divorce had only happened three months ago. To further that point, I was a just a month past my head injury; one that came with a natural side effect of heightened emotions and loss of control over those emotions at times. She made me feel better. Maybe I was being too hard on myself. Maybe we all are, at times, too hard on ourselves and expect too much from ourselves. I forced myself to remember that everything happens for a reason and everything happens in God's time. I wonder what his plan is.

Dear God, please help me grow stronger and more fit each day. Please help me grow spiritually, mentally, and physically. Please watch over all my family, extended and future. Please keep us all safe, healthy, and happy for as long as possible. Please help me to live out your plan for me.

Opening my bible that night, again I pray that the Holy Spirit guides me to the pages he wants me to see. He opens Luke 1:1-4. He tells me, "Since many have undertaken to compile a narrative of the events that have been fulfilled among us, just as those who were eyewitnesses from the beginning and ministers of the word have handed them down to us, I too have decided, after investigating everything accurately anew, to write it down in an orderly sequence for you most excellent Theophilus, so that you may realize the certainty of the teachings you have received."

From this, again I am understanding that I must write this book. For anyone else that has ever suffered through a dark and trying time and has struggled to find the light. This book is for you. Ask Jesus to pick you up and carry you. This book is for any person going through or considering a divorce. Pray to God to save your marriage. These writings and these conversations are proof that God works miracles, even in this 21ˢᵗ century. The Holy Spirit is alive and well today! Believe, even for one moment that God can help you and HE will! I am writing these words today because when I was struggling in the pit of my heart, drowning in my tears, and wondering WHY? Somehow, I managed to cry out for help and Jesus heard me. I was a lost sheep and he found me. He will find you and bring you back into the fold. It will be in his way and in his time, but it will be good. I just know it. I also believe it will help you, dear reader, if you journal your own thoughts and feelings as well.

The next morning, on the way to church for Sunday mass, I heard the "cody-bird" whistling. I do not know what the real name of the bird is; it's a bird that my ex-husband used to hear whistling when he was at his home as a child growing up. He said he called it the "cody-bird" because when it whistled, it sounded like it was whistling his name as it sang. When we bought our home together, his parents were with us one day when we were remodeling it and we had stopped for a break on the front porch. His mom called our attention to the "cody-bird" singing, telling us it was a sign that this home was meant to be ours because it even had our own "cody-bird." The bird chirps, "cody-bird, cody-bird, cody-bird" in this pretty little melody as if it is beckoning to you.

On September 29, I heard a "cody-bird" whistling to me way down in Florida as we were leaving the hotel that morning for church. In fact, I have heard it every day for the past three days. It must have a home perched in the tree by the pool, set up to taunt me. I have also heard that silly bird at my home in Illinois a few times too. I thought birds were supposed to sing in the spring and leave us alone in the Fall? It makes me sad. But to be honest, it also makes me feel hopeful… I know it's such a stupid pipedream to think that my husband could come back, and we could fix our broken life, but I do still think about it. Deep in my heart, if someone forced the truth to the surface, I want my Cinderella storybook ending.

However, I am supposed to go sign my annulment application papers this week when I return to Illinois. I do not know how to articulate how I feel or even how to think about this happening. I know it fills me with utter fear to think the church might annul my marriage--- the marriage that I loved every moment of. I know God loves me and has a perfect plan for me, but the doubt creeps in and I am so afraid. I do not want to be afraid. I wish I were calm and free flowing, content to wait and find out whatever God's plan has in store for me. Instead I cry fat, hot tears for what I perceive as a huge loss.

Dear God, I pray I find peace and acceptance for your will. I pray you grant me serenity to accept the thing I cannot change. I pray my husband finds peace and his heart heals. I pray that your plan can come to fruition according to your will. Amen.

This night, in Isaiah 38:1-6 I am shown the reading about sickness and recovery of Hezekiah. At the end of my reading this passage I am stunned, once again, by the timing and the alignment of the reading that God shows me. It seems to align so much with my life. I do not know the bible well enough to find these readings; it must be the Holy Spirit showing me that He is watching over me and preparing to heal me and perfect me…

"In those days, when Hezekiah was mortally ill, the prophet Isaiah, son of Amoz, came and said to him: "Thus says the Lord: Put your house in order, for you are about to die; you shall not recover." Then Hezekiah turned his face to the wall and prayed to the Lord: O Lord, remember how faithfully and wholeheartedly I conducted myself in your presence, doing what was pleasing to you!" And Hezekiah wept bitterly. Then the word of the Lord came to Isaiah: "Go, tell Hezekiah: Thus, says the Lord, the God of your father David: I have heard your prayer and seen your tears. I will heal you: in three days you shall go to the Lord's temple; I will add 15 years to your life. I will rescue you and this city from the hand of the king of Assyria; I will be the shield to this city."

I re-read this, remembering I am supposed to go sign my annulment papers in three days! Is this a sign? Will I and my marriage be saved and healed? Or will I be moving on to a new life? I know it is not for me to try to analyze and figure it out ahead of time. I do think it is God giving me a sign that he is hearing my cries and seeing my tears, just like he did for Hezekiah.

The next day I received a text message from my ex-husband. To be honest, my heart did leaps when I saw his name come across the screen. Of course, my hopes were quickly dashed when I read his words. He only wanted to talk business, as was his usual style. He said he needed a copy of our previous year's tax return. Still, a part of me wanted to believe he was using that as an excuse to test the waters to contact me. My head knows that is a silly wish, given all the facts. But my heart wants what my heart wants...

That night, I focus my prayers on simple thanks. *Dear God, thank you for not giving up on me. Thank you for loving me and blessing my life (even though the last year has been so hard). Please help me gain wisdom so that I may choose wisely and follow your plan for my life. You know what is best for me and what is truly my heart's desire.* I think if we each stop and thank God for something each day our lives will be better for it.

1 Maccabees 1:25-28 tells me "And there was great mourning for Israel, in every place they dwelt, and the rulers and the elders groaned. Virgins and young men languished, and the beauty of the woman was disfigured. Every bridegroom took up lamentation, she who sat in the bridal chamber mourned. And the land was shaken on account of its inhabitants, and all the house of Jacob was covered with shame."

To me, this reading says that both my husband and I are hurting. Even though he brought about all these changes and demanded that we divorce, the man that I married must be in there somewhere and hurting too. God does not want divorce for anyone. My husband was baptized and chosen by God to be one of his people. Therefore, he too is protected by God's mantle. He must be hurting. When people choose to divorce it hurts so many, how can we all (not just my husband and I) recover from this travesty?

17

Show Some Faith

October second-- What a day! We were traveling back from our trip and I cried from Memphis, Tennessee to Springfield, Illinois. This time silent tears just streamed down my cheeks. I was dreading my annulment appointment later that day, thoughts of my marriage kept swirling in my head, and doubts about my new relationship with the man from Missouri would not leave me alone.

Sitting down to talk to Deacon Victor about my annulment application made me feel like a quitter and a fake. I felt like I was asking God to let me out of my promise to be married to my husband until death do us part. I know I kept my promise and he did not. I know that the responsibility lies on him for our break-up. I also know that God knows my heart and has a perfect plan for my life. I have put it in his hands now completely. I must, I've done everything I knew to try. He will guide me and provide for me. If our marriage is to be annulled, then it is up to God to tell me that it was never a sacramental union and then I will be able to accept that and finally have peace.

After my meeting with Deacon, I went to church. I prayed for strength, courage, and wisdom. I lit a candle for my husband. I prayed that his heart would be healed and for God's will to be done. There is truly nothing earthly left for me to do but TRUST in God.

This day was also the feast day of the Guardian Angels. I offered special prayers for my guardian angel, whom I believe is called Danielle. I thanked Danielle for being such a good guardian angel to me. I also asked "her" to talk to my husband's angel and the angel that watched over the man from Missouri. I asked that the angels watch over and guide these two men that they may be safe and guided to make good choices. I also offered prayers of thanks to God for this vacation time I had with my parents. I love them so much and they are such wonderful parents!

Dear God, you know what is best for me and my life. You know what is in my heart but also what I need. Please fill me with trust and faith in you and in my future. Thank you for every blessing you have given me—even the ones I do not recognize as blessings. Please tell me what I need to know to keep going and improving my life.

2 Maccabees 12-17: Now I beg those who read this book not to be disheartened by these misfortunes, but to consider that these chastisements were meant not for the ruin but for the correction of our nation. It is, in fact, a sign of great kindness to punish sinners promptly instead of letting them go for long...He never withdraws his mercy from us...he does not abandon his own people. Let these words suffice for recalling this truth."

My younger sister is getting married this month. But I am so tired today. I am tired physically, mentally, and emotionally. I am tired of waiting and wondering and stressing and crying over it all. I am tired of pretending to be strong. I am just spent.

The man from Missouri is coming down to be my date for my sister's wedding. Honestly, I do not know if I want him to come. I am so tired and stressed it seems like more work. I'm worried about having to help him get here, play hostess while he's here, explain why I have to spend so much time away from him because I am the maid of honor in my sister's wedding, etc. etc. I have always thought that if something were meant to be it would be easy. This does not seem easy to me. Of course, nothing seems easy right now...

My mind is so messed up...I literally start having a silent conversation with God: *Dear God, I am such a mess! Please save me from myself! What do I do? I need a plan… Something to work on or plan for… Can you help me find guidance? Proverbs 17:22 "A joyful heart is the health of the body, but a depressed spirit dries up the bones."*

Yes, God. I know. But how do I find joy and not be depressed?

Sirach 30:23 "Distract yourself, renew your courage, drive resentment far away from you; for worry has brought death to many, nor is there ought to be gained from resentment."

In my mind, I hear an interior voice say in plain words to me *"Find a way to be happy CeCe. You are blessed with much around you."* I should have taken the time in that moment to listen and list all my blessings again. (Should you do that now?)

Another message comes through to me at church on October sixth. It was about having faith even when things look like they are the worst possible scenario. It says in the bible and today's reading that if we had faith as small as a mustard seed and we told the mulberry tree to uproot and plant itself in the ocean it would obey our command! It says this would happen because that is how strong our faith would be—even if it was as little as a tiny mustard seed! Isn't that amazing? Here I am crying and pouting and asking for courage and all I really must do is have a little tiny bit of faith! God has given me signs all through this process that he will provide. Now I just must believe and show some faith!

Dear Mary, Mother of God, please pray with me that I will grow in faith and exercise it like you did. Yours was a terrible, frightening, painful situation but you still said, "let it be done unto me according to God's will." Hail Mary full of grace, the Lord is with you. Blessed art thou amongst women and blessed is the fruit of thy womb, Jesus. Holy Mary, Mother of God, pray for us sinners now and at the hour of our death. Amen. Immaculate heart of Mary, pray for us sinners now and at the hour of our death. Immaculate heart of Mary, pray for us sinners now and at the hour of our death. {Here I prayed for my father-in-law and my husband.}

My sister's wedding day was here! She looked beautiful and was so happy. Her husband is an absolute gem and the wedding went off without a hitch. I had prayed that I would not break down in tears during the wedding ceremony or the reception and God blessed me with the courage, love, and wisdom to enjoy the day. He even inspired me with the right words to include during my maid-of-honor speech. Somehow, I was able to realize that the day was not about me or my situation, even though it was full of reminders.

My sister was married in the same church that blessed my parents' marriage more than 40 years previously. It was the same church that my husband went through RCIA just two years prior. The same church I attended weekly mass. As I walked down the aisle as a bridesmaid in my sister's wedding, I couldn't help but wonder if my ex-husband and I had said our vows in this church if things had turned out differently for us. I know it was a random thought that had no bearing on the outcome of the truth in our marriage, but it was the way of my thoughts in those days.

The way of my "ex-husband's" thoughts just a few days prior to my sister's wedding were continuing to be those of a stranger to me. I had reached out to him, called him on the telephone, to ask him if he would meet me to discuss the paperwork involved surrounding the annulment I was seeking. He flat out refused. He told me to send it to him. He said he could read. When I tried to explain to him that I knew that he could read, but that this process was important to me and that he hadn't been Catholic for very long and I just wanted to be sure he was clear on the process that it entails. Besides that, I reminded him that he had promised in our divorce decree that he would cooperate with this church paperwork since I had cooperated as much as I could with the signing of all his wanted paperwork. His next words took me by surprise because he yelled at me, letting me know in no uncertain terms that what I was asking for was just an inconvenience for him! Of course, I ended up in tears at the end of this conversation. After all the years, the happiness and joys we had shared together I had been reduced to nothing more than an inconvenience to him.

Of course, these thoughts were rattling around in my brain at my sister's wedding too, but with God's grace I managed to squash them well and be in her moments. Her day was perfect. Father Amobi, who had walked my husband through RCIA, officiated my sister's wedding and had beautifully crafted and profound words for her and her husband, but also for me too. I listened intently as he explained in his homily about 1 Corinthians 1-13. He explained what love is and what love is not. Love is patient. Love is kind. It is not jealous or cruel. Father Amobi's homily made me realize that if my husband really had any love left for me, he would have found a way to keep his promise to me. He would have NEVER be so cruel to me, no matter what else was going on or what he was going through. It helped my mind calm to think of this. It helped me get through that day and future days to come. In those moments after I realize this, I offer thanks to God for the many blessings he has given me and my family. I ask that He help guide me to be the best person I can be.

When I got back to my bible after my sister's wedding, I find in Baruch 6:72, "The better for the just man who has no idols: He shall be far from disgrace!" I back up my reading to Baruch 5:21-23 and find even more meaningful words. "Fear not my children; call upon God, who will deliver you from oppression at enemy hands. I have trusted in Eternal God for your welfare, and joy has come to me from the Holy One because of the mercy that will swiftly reach you from your eternal savior. With mourning and lament I send you forth, but God will give you back to me with enduring gladness and joy. In verse 27 he says, "Fear not, my children; call out to God! He who brought this upon you will remember you. As your hearts have been disposed to stray from God, turn now 10 times the more to seek him; for he who has brought disaster upon you will, in saving you, bring you back enduring joy."

See, God is telling me (and others like me) that I just have to stay the course. Stay true to my trust in God. He does not want me to suffer; he will bring the joy back to my life. I know it will be true, I just have to be patient... Of course, I am human. Any reader can testify to my struggles. It is hard! As a human, I want things to be easy, I do not relish in the struggle while I'm in the middle of it. I can recognize that I should be learning from it, if I stay focused and true there could be good that comes from it... TRUST... I must remember my image from before, like the footprints in the sand poem. I know Jesus will carry me, even when I think I'm the one doing all the hard work… he's really the one winning the battle for me…

The more I think about all the family time I have been given, the more I realize and appreciate what a blessing it has been. Once I stop struggling against this thought that I have to get back to work as quick as I can and surrender to the fact that I am not in control of how fast my body will heal, I allow myself to relax and rest: emotionally and physically allow myself to feel a calm come over me for one day. It has been ten days since my sister got married and today feels like a good day! I am grateful for the relaxation. My parents even stop by to take me to McDonalds, which is not a huge deal, but when you can't drive a trip to anywhere is appreciated! It is during this drive that I realize this extra family time is so important. What a blessing.

I give silent thanks to God for blessing me a wonderful family and a close circle of friends. Even through this painful time, I have been so blessed by love and support, especially from my family. I love them so much! In 2 Chronicles 4:7 I am shown the verse, "He made the lampstands of gold, ten of them as was prescribed, and placed them in the nave, five to the right and five to the left." I am not entirely sure, but I think this is one part in the bible where Solomon is readying the temple? Am I readying my own temple?

18

Everything Happens for a Reason

I was awoken at almost 2 in the morning by my dad calling me on my cell phone. He told me he thought my mom had a stroke and he was taking her to St. Monica's hospital. I took his words, stayed calm because that is what I was supposed to do, and waited for my brother to come pick me up. While we raced to the hospital, I called my two sisters and another brother to let them know what little I knew and where we were headed. Of course, they would be shortly behind us.

Once in the emergency room, it was decided that I would go into the admitting room with my mother. My dad does not hear well at all, my brother would wait with him. My sister who works in a hospital setting wasn't there yet, so I was it-- brain injury or no.

Mom was not really lucid. She was unable to answer simple questions like what day was it? Who was the president of the United States? Where are you? Every five minutes she kept announcing the time she would see on the clock on the wall. Then she would ask me what happened? "It's 2:45? What happened? It is 2:50? What happened?" This was so terrifying! I started praying the Hail Mary right away and asking God to watch over my mother. It was the only thing that I had only power over and the only thing that I could think of to do. Plus, it kept me somewhat calm and kept my mind from swirling into "worst case scenario mode."

Hours later, when the results of all the testing came through, it was discovered that my mom had indeed suffered a stroke. There are these events like mini strokes, called transient cerebral ischemia (TIA). This was an attack caused by a loss of blood flow in the brain. She had been at home, helping one of her dog's birth puppies. Something went terribly wrong with the dog and the birth, which was way too stressful for my mom. In truth, it was probably the proverbial straw that broke the camel's back. Given the preceding year's stress with my heartbreak, divorce, my head injury, then the unintended stress of my sister's wedding, then the death of one of the family's pets must have thrown her over the edge.

While my mom spent a few days in the hospital recuperating from this TIA, I could not help but ponder if this was yet another form of spiritual attack against us in the year of the family. I know God pulls you closer in times of need and will work all things to the good. I decided to focus on the good, because that is what will defeat all else in the end.

Dear God, thank you for once again watching over and protecting our family. Mary, Mother of God, thank you for praying for my mom. Holy Trinity, thank you for once again proving that you are on our side and guiding us. Please continue to strengthen our faith and help us to be worthy of your love.

I find my answer in 2 Kings 3:23-27. "This is blood! They exclaimed... the Israelites rose up and attacked the Moabites, who fled from them... The wrath against Israel was so great that they gave up the siege and returned to their own land..."

A few days after my mom's episode, she was released from the hospital. Yay! Thanks to God for his mercy! I am still out of work. My doctor said it would be another month, maybe sooner if the new meds he put me on started working and healing me faster. I begin to think there must be some reason that I am not released to go back to normal yet. Do I need more rest? Should I pursue this book idea? Spend more time with family? Probably yes to all three. I definitely need to refocus on healthy eating, maybe lose some more weight.

Again, I feel God talking to me through my bible. Today he spoke to me through Matthew 11:23, "...For if the mighty deeds done in your midst had been done in Sodom, it would have remained until this day." And also, in verse 28, "Come to me, all you who labor and are burdened, and I will give you rest."

I feel like he is saying to me-- there you have it, CeCe. I am giving you a sign. Like the one my husband had asked for: one as big as a billboard! God is working miracles for you, pay attention. All I have to do is receive his message and rest. For now, ...

The following Saturday night my good friend Amy comes to get me, and I go with her and her husband to a euchre party just down the road from my house at her cousin's place. I did not know anyone at the party, but it was fun to be out and about. My friend was sharing with me the details about her cousin, whose party we were at, who had a wife who he still loves and wants her back, even though she left him. I felt for him in his situation. He was trying to live a normal life, despite his apparent heart break. It reminded me that no one had a perfect life, that it is easy to get lost in your own misery and think you're all alone. I am continually reminded that I have wonderful family and friends—true friends! I am very blessed.

That night, upon returning home I pray to God, thanking him for my blessings. *Dear God, please continue to heal my heart, my mind, and my body. Thank you for all the blessings you have bestowed upon me. I know you love me, and I hope I can continue to increase my faith and be the best person I can be.*

Through 2 Maccabees 5:19-20 I find the Lord speaking to me. "The Lord, however, had not chosen the people for the sake of the Place, but the Place for the sake of the people. Therefore, the Place itself, having shared in the people's misfortunes, afterward participated in their good fortune; and what the Almighty had forsaken in his anger was restored in all its glory, once the Sovereign became reconciled." Somehow, I feel that in this instance I am the PLACE. I was, for tonight, allowed to share in someone else's misfortunes so that I could have a greater understanding that I am not alone in my misfortunes-- this PLACE I am in the midst of.

This gives me even more drive and determination to share my story with others. Half of all marriages end in divorce nowadays. There is a nation full of people that must be hurting like me. When I was crying and struggling to drive into work most days, searching for something that would help me I wished there was a book that I could turn to that would let me know what to do next, or how to get grip on myself. This book may or may not be that, but I hope that it helps someone to realize that they are not alone. There are many of us in this world of hurt called divorce, maybe like me, we did not choose to be here. Regardless it is what we choose in the process that can be the light that pulls us out of the darkness. I chose Jesus. I cried out to him and begged him to carry me. That is the reason I am writing this. Because he helped me, I hope this writing can help you.

On October twentieth I believe I had a revelation. I know what I want! I want to be happy. It sounds simple, I know. But I want to be over-the-moon, cannot wait to get home, run into the arms of my love, and smile and kiss him, happy! I want to be so attached at the hip that we are not embarrassed because we love each other so much. Does that even exist in real life? Could it exist for me? I thought I had it with my husband… There must have been a missing piece in that relationship or else it would not have failed.

Dear God, please help me find the real deal.

Again, the Lord answers me. Although, at the time I must admit, I wasn't sure to the extent what his answer really meant in Ezekiel 36:23. "I will prove the holiness of my great name, profaned among the nations, in whose midst you have profaned it. Thus, the nations shall know that I am the Lord, says the Lord God, when in their sight I prove my holiness through you." A little further in Ezekiel 36:37, "Thus says the Lord God: This also I will be persuaded to do for the house of Israel: to multiply them like sheep."

On October twenty-third, I received the first letter from the Tribunal regarding my request for the annulment of my marriage. The judge reviewing the case feels that I may have grounds for an annulment so it will be sent forward for a review. I had to sign and send back some papers, then they will send requests to my witnesses and my husband, asking for details and responses to many questions regarding the history of our courtship and overall relationship.

It breaks my heart all over again to think none of my marriage was real. But I convince myself to let it go and let God. I remind myself if I had the faith of a mustard seed I would not be crying right now. If I had faith, I would be looking forward to a future that God has planned for me. He is perfect and wants the best for me. I offer a silent prayer: *Please God, strengthen my faith and help me release my pain.*

I turn to my bible again for support. I am hoping to read the passage from Jeremiah about God knowing the plans he has for me... instead I read Matthew 26:69-75. This is the part about Peter's denial of Jesus! Oh man... I continue reading into Matthew 27:9-10. "Then was fulfilled what had been said through Jeremiah the prophet, "And they took the 30 pieces of silver, the value of a man with a price on his head, a price set by some of the Israelites, and they paid it out for the potter's field just as the Lord had commanded me."

Not exactly the reading from Jeremiah that I was looking for, I must admit. Further proof that I was not intentionally finding places in the bible to read to make myself feel better! This reading is dismal, it makes me think that in fact my marriage is dead. First, I doubt God, like Peter denied Christ, then I am throwing my marriage away into the grave, like it is worth next to nothing. But the last few words say, "...as the Lord commanded me." So, I'm supposed to bury the marriage, right? Put it behind me?

Easier said than done. I cried throughout my sleep last night. I dreamt of my husband, but upon waking I could not remember any of the details. My eyes were crusted over when I woke, and my emotions continued to be on the brink throughout the day. In my mind, I know the marriage is over; maybe this is the acceptance stage of grief. It is a terrible, terrible feeling, let me tell you! I want to be happy; I want to accept God's plan for me and allow the time it needs for it to be able to kick in, whatever it is. I know if I can do this it will all be worth it in the end, somehow. Right now, however, my future seems bleak as if I have nothing to look forward to. In 1 Kings 3:5, In Gibeon the Lord appeared to Solomon in a dream at night. God said, "Ask something of me and I will give it to you." Solomon asked for understanding to know what is right to help judge and lead God's people. In verse 10, "The Lord was pleased that Solomon made this request… In verse 12 God tells Solomon, "I do as you requested. I give you a heart so wise and understanding…" In addition, God gives him riches, glory, and a long life. I interpret this as a message of sorts, telling me to hang on, let God work for me. I know it also says in the bible somewhere that He makes all things to the good again. For now, I sit and wait. As patiently as I know how.

For several days I awake with dry tears on my face. They are the remnants of bitter dreams leftover from the nights before. My mother-in-law sent me a text near the end of October. I think she was hurting nearly as much as I was. In her text message she told me how little she is seen her son since we broke up. She told me she thinks he does not want to be happy because he had it with me and threw it all away! As much as I agree with her, as much as I love her, as much as I wish I could do or say something to make things different, I cannot. I have tried and it didn't work. For now, I know I just have to focus on me and moving my life forward. Period.

The next day was a good day. I went shopping and out to dinner with my mom. We talked, we shopped, we ate. It was a genuinely nice, comfortable day. I am very thankful for the time with her. I am trying to take each day and appreciate it for its specific value. Like today had great value for its sunshine and the time I spent with my mom. I want to be able to identify the beauty within each moment if I can. I am lucky to be alive and I want to appreciate that! My mom told me today that the doctor told her (and me, but I do not remember this) that I "escaped death" with my head injury. I really must let the impact of those words sink in. I think when you are the person that is the victim of the injury of the illness, at least in my case, you don't really truly comprehend in the moments what is happening or how gravely injured you are. I know I did not. Even when they were gluing the electrodes to my head to capture my brain waves in order to gauge the impact of the seizures or if there even were seizures, I did not understand why or what this all meant. When I spent days and nights in the hospital waiting for the swelling in my brain to go down while the doctors contemplated sawing my head open to alleviate the growing pressure, I never once stopped to consider the fact that I could die.

Even now, writing these words and thinking back to that time, it seems surreal to me. Like I was an outsider just watching a scene from a movie. I remember my mother and father-in-law coming to see me in the hospital. I remember my mother-in-law describing to me how upset she was when she read the title of the floor when they left the elevator: Neurology and Brain Trauma Center. Now it makes sense to me why my closest friends were rushing to the hospital to see me and why my younger sister barely left my side. Putting all the pieces together now, knowing the true gravity of the situation makes it even more unforgiveable that my husband—ex or not-- didn't come to see me, ask my sister, his boss about me, or inquire from his parents about how I was. He never extended any kindness or personal thought to me or anyone else close to me. It was like he never even knew me. That is not even understandable to me, much less human. Even though it hurts to think he is so far removed from the person I knew, I still wish and pray for his parent's sake that he can one day be healed.

Again, God is good to me as he comforts me with the words of Matthew 10:26-27. "Therefore, do not be afraid of them. Nothing is concealed that will not be revealed, nor secret that will not be known. What I say to you in darkness, speak in the light…"

Over the course of the next two days my emotions once again enjoy a rollercoaster ride of ups and downs. I received paperwork from the Tribunal to let me know that the witnesses I asked to participate in my annulment would get questionnaires as well as my ex-husband. Today in my heart, I feel that he is not coming back to me. I need to close that chapter of my life and move forward. With Jesus' support and the grace of God to help me I will be happy again. I just know it!

I also speak with my younger sister about the annulment. For the first time, I realize how much she is hurting in this process too. She told me she wished she could just say good riddance! She wished she could say everyone thought my husband was a terrible person who deserved to go, but she could not say that. She told me she and everyone thought we were perfect together. She affirmed my thinking that it was not just me that was blindsided when he left-- the entire family was shocked! She said she loved him like a brother, but she hated that she had to see him every day at work. She hated that she could not retaliate for me or make it all better.

I appreciated hearing her perspective. I think she would tell me the truth, even if it was something I did not want to hear. That's the way our sisterly relationship was truth first, feelings later. Even though it made me feel good for a moment, it made me question all over again why did he have to break? Why did I get to love him for only 10 years? Why couldn't we have children and the perfect life? Of course, my heart is still broken, and I don't know if it'll ever feel better.

In my readings that night, I find another affirmation that perhaps my story is somehow meant to help others too. Acts 20:35 tells me, "In every way I have shown you that by hard work of that sort we must help the weak, and keep in mind the words of the Lord Jesus who himself said, 'It is more blessed to give than to receive.'"

The first few days of November are filled with thoughts of my man from Missouri. He truly is a wonderful, good-hearted man. I love how attentive and loving he is to me. That is really who and what I need. I am excited to see him again; I want to jump in the car and drive the hours away, but alas, I have not yet been cleared to drive. However, I am realizing that I must focus on the future and make plans to enjoy my life-- whatever life it is that is in God's plan. I cannot allow myself to look back anymore. In Judith 14:9, I find solace in the words, "When she finished her account, the people cheered loudly, and the city resounded with shouts of joy." It makes me think that I am right in my thinking: The past is the past.

I have always believed that everything happens for a reason. Letting go and letting God is not easy, but I remember the faith of a mustard seed story in the bible and I am encouraged to trust in God. I feel like Mary, our Mother of God, is pulling for me too. I know she is a strong intercessor for me. 1Maccabees 2:64 reminds me in my reading, "Children! Be courageous and strong in keeping the law, for by it you shall be glorified." At church today I cried again, but I felt as if it was Jesus opening my heart to new possibilities and to a future filled with hope.

PART

THREE

19

❦

Another Miracle

In early November, I received a phone call that changed my life forever. I mean, one would think that a heartbreaking divorce and a life-threatening head injury would be enough for one person during a calendar year, but in terms of game changers, with this one phone call I was about to hit the trifecta.

I was in the passenger side of my brother's car on the interstate, making our way down to Florida. He was going down to visit a friend from high school and do some serious fishing. I had been invited to tag along once again because of my head injury. I was still off work and could not do much else, so I happily chose sunshine, sand, and warm weather over gray November days in Illinois.

A friend of a friend, who had "been in our circle" for the entire time my husband and I had been dating and married was on the other end of this phone call. As expected, there was light chit-chat for a few minutes before she told me she wanted to ask me a serious question. I said, okay? She explained that she was aware of the infertility issues that my marriage had and that she knew my ex had divorced me. I confirmed this, wondering where this conversation was going...

She continued, "You've been on my mind for months, and I've been

ng to call you, but Becky said you wouldn't be interested after
e lost adoption you went through, but I just couldn't stop thinking
about you and I just have to ask you myself and if you're not interested
I understand…" At this her voice trailed off for a moment and I sat up
straight in the car seat, wondering if I was correctly guessing where she
was trying to lead.

"It's okay, of course you can always call me…" I prompted her, not
knowing what else to say, hoping she would continue, but not really
knowing with what words she was going to continue.

"Well, I'm pregnant." She said. "And I want to ask if you will adopt
my baby."

Tears sprang to my eyes immediately. Her question really sounded
more like a plea, but she followed it up with the reasoning that she had
it on her heart to ask me for a long time but our friend had told her that
since I was recently divorced and had suffered through the loss of the
adoption with my then husband now probably wasn't a good time to ask
me. She told me that she had met with two other couples, but she couldn't
get me out of her head. She even told me at one point she had considered
terminating the pregnancy but at the last moment had not gone through
with it. In the covering of the dark car, I hid more tears from my brother
as he was driving, oblivious to the life-changing conversation happening
right beside him.

I told my friend thank you for calling me. I told her that I was
definitely interested in doing this. I explained that I was in a car on my
way to Florida for a week. I asked her if we could meet when I got back
and discuss everything face-to-face? She agreed readily, then she dropped
another bomb: the baby was due at the end of the month! I swallowed,
trying to absorb that timeline, and instead told her that I would call her
the next day and we would begin sorting out more details then. She
agreed and we hung up the phone.

I was lost in silent thoughts for several minutes after that. I was
floored. This is not a normal event. People do not just call you up on
the phone and ask you to adopt their baby—a baby that is due in a few

weeks! I had been through one lost adoption; could I so readily agree to set myself up for another potential heartbreak? Was she serious? Would she really go through with it? Could she go through with it? Could I? I was just recovering from a major head injury, hadn't even been back to work yet; should I even be considering the stress of starting a family, much less doing it on my own—a single mom this time?

As soon as these thoughts zipped through my head, a bigger even bolder thought surfaced. I asked God if this was his plan. *"Dear God if you want me to adopt this baby I will. I will do my best. I will raise him/her Catholic with love and devotion. If this is not your will, please save my heart from more pain and take it away from my path sooner rather than later. I pray this baby is healthy—whether it is mine or my friend's. Amen.*

That night in the reading of my bible, I was shown this passage from 1 Kings 13:17 "Come home with me for some refreshment," the king invited the man of God, "and I will give you a present."

Of course, as was my style, I called my mom several times over the course of the next few days. We discussed the situation ad nauseum. She allowed me to rattle on and on about every possible good or bad scenario I could think of. When I had exhausted even myself, she simply asked, "Are you done? Do you wanna know what I think?" Of course, I said yes. She simply said, "Do it."

This was what my ears had been wanting to hear! This is what my heart had already decided to do, but my head needed encouragement from my always right mother. As soon as I heard those words from her, my face erupted into a huge smile and my heart lifted with excitement that I had not allowed myself to feel yet. I was absolutely doing this! God was offering me a gift and I was running to it with open arms!

Over the next few weeks, I started planning for a future with a baby in the house. I still had many items still packed away from when the last baby was almost home. I located the crib, the pack-in-play, the blankets, and looked online for a dresser that doubled as a diaper changing table. I did not set up anything yet, as I remember all too keenly how painful it had been to tear the nursery down twice before. I was going to wait until this baby was really coming home before I got too excited about anything. I told myself this repeatedly over the next several days.

I did, however, hire an adoption attorney and start the proceedings for my home study to begin with the county adoption registry process. They all agreed that it could be somewhat "fast-tracked" since the biological mother had "found" me and agreed with everything. I was also able to start back to work on November eighteenth. A solid 12-weeks after my accident and I was back to work! Wow! It was exhausting.

I prayed daily to God that if this baby were meant to be mine then He would let it be done according to His will. He told me through scripture, 1 Corinthians 16:13-14, "Be on your guard, stand firm in the faith, be courageous, be strong. Your every act should be done with love."

As busy as I was planning and hoping for the arrival of my new baby, this time was not without further angst and heartbreak. Just before Thanksgiving, I found out that my ex-husband had moved in with the woman he left me for. His mother told me that he had not seen or talked to his parents since September, when they brought him the pie for his birthday. This made me sad all over again. I asked his mom to try to forgive him and bring him back into the family even if she had to pretend for a while. I hurt for how much pain they were in and I felt guilty because I brought them the news of our troubles. I needed their help and I thought he would listen to them once they found out what was going on. I just wanted our family to heal then and I still wanted their family to heal now. I love them so much and they don't deserve this treatment, or this hurt. *Dear God, please help their family to heal. Please watch over them, keep them safe, healthy, and show them your love.*

Psalm 41: 2-4 reads "Happy those concerned for the lowly and poor, when misfortune strikes, the Lord delivers them. The Lord keeps and preserves them, makes them happy in the land, and does not betray them to their enemies. The Lord sustains them on their sickbed, allays the malady when they are ill." Having been shown this reading right after my prayers for his family gave me great comfort.

Thanksgiving bring alternating bouts of turmoil and headstrong decision-making. My man from Missouri is not entirely convinced that he's "into the adoption idea." He keeps telling me how hard it is to raise a baby, how much money it will cost over the life of the child, and how much time it takes. He says that we are of the age now that we can travel and do whatever we want, whenever we want to do it. If I have a child that will change everything, he says.

These words sound so selfish to my ears! In fact, they sound so much like my ex-husband that I can hardly believe it. I spent 10 years with a man trying to make him happy, I put his needs and desires before my own. There were six of those years wasted trying to convince him that having a family was a good idea. Am I the one in the wrong? How can this same situation come up for me twice in two years? I feel like I am repeating the past. I want one thing and my man does not. All the while, I pray to God to lead me in the right direction, to do his will, and here I sit, crying all over again!

Dear God, what am I supposed to do? Ezekiel 21:32 answers me, "Twisted, twisted, twisted I will leave it; it shall not be the same until he who comes who has the claim against the city; and to him I will hand it over." I read these words and wonder, *"Who has the claims against the city? Am I the city? I feel like I am the city. Or is the child the city and I am the only one who can claim the child?* Maybe it is my second thought here. I am the only one that has the power, nay the RIGHT to make this decision. It is between me and God. I did not go looking for this child, but I am ready and willing to accept this gift should God choose to make it his will for me. Like Mary with her fiat, I choose to let this be done to me according to God's will!

Thanksgiving 2013 has a different feel to it than last year. Last year I had Thanksgiving dinner at the casino with a few thousand of my closest gambling strangers. This year, looking forward to the potential call about a baby on the way, I decided to pick up my old tradition of having my family over to celebrate the traditional turkey dinner, full of thanks holiday.

Of course, there were pockets full of memories of Thanksgiving past, this was the house my husband and I renovated together, and we had celebrated seven other family turkey day dinners there together. However, this day had a hopeful spark about it. I knew at any moment my phone could ring with the news that my baby could be being born! I kept imagining being in the motions of pulling the giant turkey out the oven and hearing the phone ring, rushing over to the counter, dropping the roasting pan down in a hurry, pushing the talk button on the telephone, hearing the voice on the other end say, "Come to the hospital! It's happening!" and me running out the door leaving my family to fend for themselves.

These thoughts allowed me to sweep aside those other thoughts of gray that were trying to creep in and bring me down. I could feel there was a new tide turning and I was just on the cusp of it. My man from Missouri had come around on his opinion of adopting the baby. He told me he loved me and would support my decision. He said he wanted to be with me no matter what. That was another fact that made celebrating that day even brighter.

December seventh was my parent's anniversary. Forty-some years before they had said "I-do" to each other. In all the good times and bad times, they had managed to stick together and raise five kids and survive all that life had thrown at them. That could be considered a miracle. Little did I know when I awoke that morning, another miracle was about to take place...

My baby was born the same day that is my parent's anniversary. He was perfect: ten fingers, ten little toes, dark brown hair, and he did not even cry when they poked him for their many tests! Up until the moment they wheeled him into the nursery room I had never once considered that something could even be wrong with him! Just before he appeared before me in the window, I turned to his bio-mom's boyfriend and asked, "Is he okay?" That was the first moment that fear had crept in for a split second. Up until that moment I had been rock solid in my faith, knowing that whatever God had planned for me would be fine. Her boyfriend answered me, confirming this new baby was perfect.

They asked me what I wanted to name my baby. His birthmother and I had discussed what my thoughts on names were and she liked my choices. My baby's biological mom had agreed to allow me to name him from the start, so there would be no need for name changes later or confusion about what his name was. This beautiful baby boy was 8 pounds 4 ounces, 19 inches long, and 100 percent blessing, whose name means fiery one. Every moment I looked upon him, I was overcome with the wonder of how I could be a part of such an amazing miracle. There I was, in the hospital room with a young woman who had just given birth to this bundle of pure goodness, and I was holding him, feeding him, and gazing upon him in awe. I had never felt such a powerful, encapsulating circle of grace before.

That night when I finally went home to rest, I opened my bible and thanked the Lord for the many blessings he is given me my whole life up to and especially including those moments in the hospital tonight. Thank you, God! I want to shout. If this is your will Lord, I accept it. If it's not, I will accept that too... In 2 Kings 2:3 I am answered. "...Keep still."

Three days later the unbelievable happened. My son came home with me! Thank you, God for this blessing!

Whenever I wonder about the miracles of God's plan and stop to remember how this all had to happen in an exact order, it is mind-boggling to me. There are so many factors that play in... I had to meet my ex-husband and marry him to be a part of the circle of friends to gain the trust of this wonderful young mother who would give birth to my son. My ex-husband and I would have to suffer through infertility and miscarriages to have hearts open to the thought of adoption. We had to have lost the adoption prior in order to have room in the house and more hurt in our minds, that eventually caused his destruction of our home, that made me single and available to my future son. But then, listen to these next events...

After the birth of my son, my mother told me this most interesting story: My parents travel back and forth from Illinois to Florida periodically throughout the year as they have property they enjoy in Florida, along the Gulf. At times, they take detours from their usual route and stop at Mother Angelica's shrine or other such churches. On this particular journey home to Illinois, they got stuck in a traffic jam near Huntsville, Alabama. According to my mom, my dad NEVER turns around on a road trip, but on this day he did. In an effort to get away from the stopped traffic, or maybe because of the pull of the Holy Spirit, or a combination of both, my dad turned the car around and headed towards a beautiful Catholic Church not too far off the beaten path.

After mass, they were approached by a woman carrying a small prayer card and pamphlet. This woman asked my mother if she would adopt an unborn baby in spiritual prayer. When my mother inquired further, the woman explained that this would require her to pray every day for an unborn baby that was at risk of being aborted. My mother accepted this opportunity and took the prayer card.

My mother admitted to me that she felt a little daunted by this task. Daily prayer for an unborn baby was a huge responsibility! I totally understood. I shared with my mom that my son's birthmother had considered the alternative to life for him. She had even scheduled an appointment... Thank God for her sister who refused to transport her! And thank God for my mother and her daily prayers! You see, we believe—my mother and I—that the unborn child that she prayed for daily, is my baby. We believe that her daily prayers were answered when my son's birth mom not only chose life for him but chose to reach out and contact me. Even furthering this miracle by standing firm in her decision to gift him to me through adoption. We believe that God sometimes shows off his miracles through the magic of numbers. Why else would my son be born past his due date? So, God could show off his splendor by delivering him to us on my parents' anniversary: December seventh!

20

How Could You?

By the end of December, I am realizing what a whirlwind it is to have a baby in the house. I am so busy, but so incredibly happy with my decision. It is so wonderful to rush home from work again, now to a cooing, loving baby that is so innocent and such a gift!

The man from Missouri was here with us for a week over the Christmas holiday. He is so good with my son. He is very loving, tender, and attentive. I think he could be a great father and husband...

One day, my mom asked me how I honestly felt about him. I thought about it for a moment and answered as honestly as I could. I told her I thought that if I had never met and married my husband then maybe I could be in love with the man from Missouri. There were still so many feelings in my heart and thoughts in my mind about my husband that were not allowing me to go head-strong into this new relationship. What I did know for certain was that I didn't want to hurt anymore, and I didn't want to be hurt again. I needed to pray about it and be open to accept God's will.

Ezekiel 36:33-38 tells me, "Thus says the Lord God: When I purify you from all your crimes, I will repeople the cities, and the ruins shall be rebuilt; the desolate land shall be tilled, which was formerly a wasteland exposed to the gaze of every passerby. This desolate land has been made into a garden of Eden…Thus… shall know that I, the Lord have rebuilt…I, the Lord, have promised, and I will do it…to multiply them like sheep…"

A month after my son came home from the hospital with me, I sit and write in my journal, realizing that this is a new year. With it, I have a new baby and a new beginning. Of course, at this point, I'm not over my husband but I am grateful for the new opportunities that God has blessed me with, and I am grateful for my family. My faith and my hopes are high and I know that God will lead me in the right direction. As I sit and collect my thoughts, I remember the verse from the song Amazing Grace: Through many dangers, toils, and snares, I have already come! Thank you, God!

A week later, I write again in my journal, "Every day as I gaze into my baby boy's face, I thank God for this miracle and blessing." It is not the miracle that I started out on this journey praying for, but it is awesome, and wonderful, and so much better than I could have ever imagined! I am so blessed by what an angel my baby is.

I find myself living day by day and trusting in God that his will be done. I believe that he knows what is best for me. Do not get me wrong, I still think about my "ex" husband every day, but I look forward to unfolding of the rest of God's plan. In Psalm 88:2-3 I find the verses that sum up my thoughts. "Lord, my God, I call out by day; at night I cry aloud in your presence. Let my prayer come before you; incline your ear to my cry." I know that God hears my heart, even better than I do. He will do what is best for me.

Another week passes and I write in my journal again because I dreamt of my husband. In the dream we were at a tailgate party and I asked him to talk. At first, he would not even look at me and acted like he didn't want to talk. But then in the dream he decided to walk with me… That is all I remember. Knowing I can do nothing else; I offer up prayers for him and get out of bed to go about my day.

My in-laws come to visit my son. My father-in-law held him. I watched him look down at my sweet baby's face and his own face softened and reflected all the love and peace that a blood grandfather could feel in that moment. It was touching. I could not help but think that all the pieces were there but one. I wondered if my in-laws were thinking what I was thinking: That their son, my ex-husband, should still be there in that house with us and that my son could have/should have been his son too.

My mother-in-law said that her son had called her and asked her how to sleep at night. He told her he can sleep from 9 p.m. to midnight but then is awake from midnight to 4am. He told her he cannot shut his thoughts off. My mother-in-law told me she wanted to tell him that was his conscience trying to talk to him, but she said she heard God tell her no. All I know is that I do not know what the future holds.

That night I pray again for my ex, his family, my family, and peace. Proverbs 7:9-27 shows me *"In the twilight, at dusk of day, at the dark of night, And lo! The woman comes to meet him, robed like a harlot, with secret designs— she is fickle and unruly, in her home her feet cannot rest; Now she is in the streets, now in the open squares...With much seductive speech she persuades him; with her smooth talk she compels him. All at once he follows her, as an ox goes to the slaughter...for many a victim has she laid low...Her house is the way to Sheol, going down to the chambers of death."*

I felt sick. I knew in my heart this was what happened. I knew my husband had somehow fallen into a snare and could not find his way out. This renewed my prayers for him, but I also knew that it was out of my hands. I would have to have faith that God would save him. I know his baptism was special, he was chosen by God and God would not abandon him. I would just have to pray that my ex-husband would someday want to turn back to God. That is all I could do.

There are so many moments when I almost believe that I am being strong. Everyone keeps telling me how strong I am, but the truth is, I am just faking it! That is how I feel on the inside anyway. There is a strong inner piece of me that is trusting in God, but there's also a strong subconscious part of me that feels like I'm just waiting for my husband to come home. I am still so teary-eyed when I think about him. I know I am holding off on moving forward with the man from Missouri because of my feelings that are still so strong for my ex-husband. For some reason, I still think he will come home to me. My heart is broken; I know I am still in shock over what he did to me. How could he? I believed 100 percent that he was the one for me and that we would be together forever! My renewed prayer is: Dear God, how do I let him go? *"I will turn you about, I will urge you on, and I will make you come up from the recesses of the north; I will lead you against the mountains of Israel."(Ezekiel 39:2).*

Within 24 hours, God's words to me were ringing true. Events occurred and words were said that turned my thinking around and spurred me on into a new direction. It is unbelievable to imagine that what I am about to share happened, but they did, and it was proof that the relationship between my husband and I was very, very broken.

It was a Saturday afternoon in late January when my ex and I got into a screaming match over the phone. In almost ten years of being together, we had never yelled at each other. This night, it was like communicating with an absolute stranger. I sent him a text message about a tax form, and he called me back, using every word he could in an effort, I believe, to try and hurt me. He told me he hated me; he never wanted to talk to me again, I was the biggest mistake of his life, and he wanted to beat me up as if I were a man.

I felt so stupid. So stupid to have kept holding out hope that the man I had married was still inside that human shell somewhere. I knew then, with no more doubts, the man I married was truly dead to me. I am done. Tonight, is the last night that I will let him hurt me. I refuse to allow myself anymore tears for him. The man I spoke to tonight is not anyone I care to ever think of again! It was as if another being was inside his body! Even his voice was distorted.

One thing he said did ring with some truth, however. After he had spat all the venom he could at me, he did admit that he was deeply sorry for the way he had treated his mother. Then in a calm and questioning voice, he went on to ask me, "How could you go and adopt a baby? Don't you know that is what broke me? That failed adoption."

126

I was dumbstruck. I did not know what to say. Of course, I knew that the failed adoption and his father's heart attack happening on the same day had affected him profoundly and caused this whole mess. How could he be harboring some resentment against me for adopting a baby that was a gift from God? I had not been actively searching or looking to adopt when my son was gifted to me. Even though the conversation was very hurtful to me, this one tiny admission from him left me with a glimmer of hope for his soul to come back to health. Someday.

Dear God, I know now I am not meant to wait for my husband to return to me. His words today cut me deeply and I know I am not strong enough to withstand any more of this. I am still sad for our loss and for the loss of us; I just pray you strengthen me in faith and courage to look to the future. I know you stand by me. 1 Kings 16: There was a war between Asa and Baasha, King of Israel, as long as they both reigned.

Weeks pass and the man from Missouri and I continued to spend time with each other. We are enjoying dating and both feeling blessed with the presence of the new baby. My home study is approved in the adoption process and things are proceeding very well in that category. The man from Missouri and I have begun to talk about getting engaged and married. I know at this point my annulment has not been approved, but maybe if we pick a date far enough out it will be by then. We begin to discuss December thirteenth, of next year as a possibility. (I still think about my ex-husband every single day, but I am trying to convince myself it was never meant to be. He has hurt me so much, maybe the best way for me to get over it and to process everything is to just forget it and move on!

I still offer a prayer to God, asking for his guidance. Dear God, is this the right path for me? The answer comes swiftly, in my mind it seems almost vehemently from Luke 13:5. *"By no means! But I tell you, if you do not repent, you will all perish as they did!"*

Well... That cannot be good. So, no new marriage is the message I am hearing. Okay... Even though this message is as plain as day to me now, I must admit that I am still a stubborn person, maybe a slow learner one might say. I did not read these words and break up with the man from

Missouri. I continued to see him, allowing my feelings to develop even more for him. He was a nice, loving man. Maybe, I thought, it was just bad timing. Maybe I was not supposed to get married, but it was okay to keep dating him? On a secular level, I did not think it was fair that I could not try to be happy or try to start my life over. It was not my fault that my husband had cheated on me and decided to abandon me and quit on our life together.

In 2 Samuel 21:16-22, "There is an ancient saying, 'Let them ask if they will in Abel or in Dan whether loyalty is finished or ended in Israel." I read this and felt like I was being told to sit still and wait. It felt like that just because we had been granted a civil divorce in the state of Illinois, we had not been awarded an annulment and in the eyes of God, we were still married. I was very torn, seemingly having placed myself in the chasm between wanting the past and not being able to have it and wishing for the future and not being ready for that either.

My son's birthmother signed the consent forms for the adoption and our judge signed the court approval forms! My son will be officially placed for adoption with me by the court system within the next few weeks and the final adoption date is set for June. I am free to schedule my blessing, my son, my miracle baby to be baptized. Praise God! Thank you, Jesus, Mary, and Joseph for praying and protecting my family. God's miracle is in place!

21

The Answer is NO

Matthew 9:15, 22, 29 seem to show me the steps that had to occur recently. It seems as if my husband had to leave me and I mourned but I had to have faith to be saved. Once I did, Jesus cured my affliction, "Can the wedding guests mourn as long as the bridegroom is with them? The days will come when the bridegroom is taken away from them, and then they will fast…Jesus turned around and saw her, and said, "Courage, daughter! Your faith has saved you!" …Then he touched their eyes and said, "Let it be done to you according to your faith."

Why do I find myself dreaming of my ex-husband again? Days before the baptism of my son and my mind is circling back to my ex? I dreamed that my ex-husband came to me and apologized for hurting me so badly. He told me he wanted to try and work it out with me. He told me that he did not love her. Right in front of me, in the dream, he broke up with her and sent her on her way. I kissed the top of his head, hugged him, and told him that I loved him. But he did not say it back. And what is more important in this dream, I realize, is that I never told him I would take him back…

By the beginning of May I was amid another cycle of near depression. I was tired in the morning and tired when I went to bed at night. Being a single mother was hard work! Don't get me wrong, I am so happy with my baby! I love him so much and am so grateful that God blessed me with him. It is just much harder to balance work and motherhood alone than I thought it would be.

My (ex) mother-in-law mailed me a Mother's Day card and gift. She is just the sweetest person alive and I love her dearly! It is hard not to let the tears flow and allow myself to think about how perfect my life could be if my husband had made different choices. I miss that side of my family and what I used to have with them and my husband so much! I know God's plan for me, and my son is wonderful. I just must trust, believe, and be PATIENT! I wonder if my ex ever wished things were different. This day, I was shown in my bible the following verse, which did give me comfort with that thought from Matthew 27:3, "Then Judas, his betrayer, seeing that Jesus had been condemned, deeply regretted what he had done."

The same thoughts must have been heavy on my mother's mind as well. It just so happened that eleven years to the day of when he proposed to me, she happened to ask me again if my husband were to come back, would I be able to tell him no? She admitted to me that part of her still hoped for that miracle: That he would come back to the way he was before and work like mad to win me back and prove he's better and try to make up for how much he's hurt me. It would be a lie for me to say I did not think about that same thing too.

Someone told me it is possible for people to change, but they do not change back. I think about that too when I think about the possibility of him coming back to me. The pain he caused me and his actions and however he truly feels about everything would still be there. Of course, I still loved the man I married, maybe I always will. I just have to TRUST in God's plan. Nothing else is in my power.

1 Samuel 18:10-12 tells a story about Saul and David [The next day an evil spirit from God came over Saul, and he raged in his house. David was in attendance, playing the harp as at other times, while Saul was holding his spear. Saul poised the spear, thinking to nail David to the wall, but twice David escaped him.] Saul began to fear David, [because the Lord was with him, but had departed from Saul himself.]

I pondered long and hard over this reading. What was I to learn from this? Again, the images of the evil one waging war against the family and marriage is the only thing that comes to mind. He hates marriage. Marriage is one of the best things here on earth. If we, as a society, allow marriage to continue to be destroyed, then I believe our foundation as loving beings is in jeopardy. God put us here on earth to learn to love each other and marriage is a sacramental way of pledging that love to each other for eternity. If I continue to fight to hold onto my marriage, as recognized by the church and by God, I am still fighting the good fight against the devil. That I can do. Until God tells me different.

By the end of May, I begin thinking about writing this book again. My hope is that someone will read it and feel more hope if they are going through a similar situation to what I went through. I have worries about sharing my innermost thoughts and fears with strangers and the world. I am a private person and fear what people close to me will think when they read everything, or even what strangers will think as they delve into my feelings and emotions. I ask God in my daily prayers if I should write this book? I believe I am answered when I turn to Acts 5:4, "While it remained unsold, did it not remain yours? And when it was sold, was it not still under your control?"

The day my son turned six-months old, I allowed myself to sit in absolute wonder of the glorious miracle that I had been blessed with being a witness to. It was so amazing to think I have been blessed with his love and existence for six months! He is made me so happy! I thank you, God for this, every day. He is a wonderful, joyful blessing! He is so perfect and magical. I never knew it would be so much hard work yet so rewarding. I am only now beginning to understand how my mother felt with five of us. Why wouldn't I want a houseful? My son is just so perfect! God is so, so good! To think, I never asked for this miracle, yet he was given to me freely. HE, our God, has saved me.

A few days later, another crazy thing happened to me. My old college sweetheart phoned me while I was at work. After 12 years of not speaking to each other, he called me up, out of the blue to apologize to me. It was so surreal. It was like an event from a movie, really. As a young adult with unrequited love I would wish for the day he would wake up and realize he made a mistake and come find me again: like the scene from Pretty Woman with Richard Gere and Julia Roberts, you know? The one where he pulls up in the limo and yells, "Vivian!" And she comes out to the balcony and asks him what he's doing there, and he answers that he's there to rescue her. Then she in turn, rescues him right back. That's the scene that my young love inspired mind conjured up whenever I envisioned this happening all those years ago.

Well, it was not quite like that, but it was good to hear an apology anyway. It made me think it was God's way of telling me that I was a good person and here was another person that could tell me that same thing! And as silly as it sounds, I did need to hear it from this guy. He was the original boy that broke my heart. He was the one that my husband reminded me of. He was the original boy that I had believed was my soulmate. After we broke up, I stopped believing in soulmates. He was the one that I always thought "got away" while at the same time my parents were sure to be thinking they were glad he got away!

It was in this simple phone call that God was yet again, giving me another gift. The gift of reconciliation. Through this phone call I was able to forgive my college love and share our current sob stories. He was in the middle of a divorce. He needed to hear that he was not such a bad guy. He needed reassurances that I could give him. I had been where he was now, and I knew his redeeming qualities. For even though years ago he had broken my heart, time had healed those scars and allowed me to see him as he was: just a boy trying to do the best he could in life's impossible situations. Just like any of the rest of us. And since I was ahead of him in this current game called the world of divorce hurt, I was uniquely qualified to come to his rescue on this current day. I could help him through this hurt. So, I tried.

Later that same day, Deacon Victor told me that my annulment paperwork was proceeding forward. He had one more paper to complete to send in then I should have an answer soon from the tribunal. What is the next phase of God's plan for me?

1 Chronicles 17:25-27 tells me, "Because you, O my God, have revealed to your servant that you will build him a house, your servant has been made bold to pray before you. Since you, O Lord, are truly God and have promised this good thing to your servant, and since you have deigned to bless the house of your servant, so that it will remain forever—since it is you, O Lord, who blessed it, it is blessed forever."

When I read these words, at the time in 2014, I was thinking that God was trying to tell me not to worry about whether my marriage would be annulled. In my mind, I still believed that he had blessed our marriage and it would remain intact. Reading these words again in 2018, I think the words mean that he has blessed me. Because I have been praying and trusting in his mercy, he is going to make me okay again.

In December of 2014, my spirits are crushed once again. It is like my life has become a rollercoaster of emotions with the only constant being the idea that I can count on being blindsided at any moment. The letter from the Diocesan Tribunal came in the mail denying my application for annulment. They said that my marriage was still valid, and I was not free to remarry. For all intents and purposes, I was held captive in my past without any hope of reprieve. Just weeks before Christmas and my spirits were crushed. What little hope I had allowed myself to begin building up was demolished with one brief letter.

Months go by, during which: I sell my married life home, move the man from Missouri up here to Illinois, buy a house in the city and all the while still manage to think of my ex-husband EVERY SINGLE DAY. I really hate how much I still think about him! I sold everything we had together that would remind me of him. I boxed up every picture and memento and have done my best to move on. It appears that my ex has moved on in every possible way; he has even gotten remarried! How long am I going to have to suffer? I have a boyfriend, yes. But often it feels like pretend, like a placeholder. My feelings for him are real, yes. But they are not the same. I can hardly make it through a day without some thought creeping into my mind, clawing and climbing its way from the trenches of my heart. It is just not fair!

My bible consoles me this day. He gives me exactly what I need to hear from Nahum 1:12, "For, says the Lord, be they ever so many and so vigorous, still they shall be mown down and disappear. Though I have humbled you, I will humble you no more. Now I will break his yoke from off you and burst asunder your bonds." This reading brings with it hope again. The hope that a divorced woman needs. Peace is coming, believers. Just wait.

In June 2015, I come home to find a turtledove trying to nest in the flower basket on my front porch. Earlier today I was thinking to God to tell me or give me some sort of sign if I am still supposed to be waiting for my ex-husband. I believe there must be a reason I am still experiencing such great heartache. And yes, my son is worth it all! Without my ex-husband, my son would not be in my life: the proper people had to cross my path to be able to put those currents in motion, I know. In my heart, I am 100 percent sure that if there was only *this* path that would lead me to then he is worth all the heartache I have endured. No question, and I would do it all again.

But then, why not allow my marriage to be annulled? It has been two years... Turtledoves mate for life, I begin to think. Did I have full knowledge of the commitment and sacrifice I was getting into when I married my ex-husband? Did the sacrament actually occur between us on our wedding day? There is only one turtledove nesting on my porch... Where is the other one? Is this meant as my sign? I know it takes two to make a true marriage, or a true sacrament work...

Then I read my bible that night: <u>The Demand for a Sign</u> "Teacher, we wish to see a sign from you." He said to them in reply, "An evil and unfaithful generation seeks a sign, but no sign will be given it except the sign of Jonah the Prophet. Just as Jonah was in the belly of the whale three days and three nights, so will the Son of Man be in the heart of the earth three days and three nights" (Matthew 12:39).

22

❦❦❦❦❦❦

Endings and Beginnings

In October 2015, I began attending Alpha at my church. There is a young woman there, somewhere around my age who also is divorced and heartbroken about her situation. I believe God put us in the same group for a reason. She is an incredibly beautiful soul and my heart feels like it is reaching out to her. I decided to share my story with her and the other ladies in the group tonight. The whole thing—from the point where my husband said he was "unhappy," to the point of my head injury, to the adoption of my son. It was cathartic for me, but I think moreover, it helped my new friend. I think it helped her realize that she is not alone in her heartache and that God will help her too.

Sharing my story with this small women's group also reminded me to keep up with my nightly prayers and to continue to reach out to the Holy Spirit for guidance. I am even praying to Mary that she prays that these knots that I have created in my life to become undone in God's time, if it is His will. In my heart of hearts, I know I should not be living with a man that is not my husband, even if I do love him and want to be married to him. Even if I am working on my annulment. The timing of it all was my time, not God's time. I know I want to be happy and I want my son to be in the best possible situation. Above all else, though, I know that God's plan is better than my plan! He has proven that time and time again. It is just about time that I start listening to him again!

2 Maccabees 5:16-17 says, "He laid his impure hands on the sacred vessels and gathered up with profane hands the votive offerings made by other kings for the advancement, the glory, and the honor of the Place. Puffed up in spirit, Antiochus did not realize that it was because of the sins of the city's inhabitants that the Lord was angry for a little while and hence disregarded the holy Place."

Isn't this saying, plain as day, to me that I was doing wrong? Not that God was leaving me, but that I was not doing what was pleasing to the Lord? That is how I read it today. If you, my friends, are reading this and question your own situation, ask yourselves, are you living according to God's plan for your life? Or are you, like me at this time in my history, taking things into your own hands and trying to make things happen according to your own will? It is a tough question to ask, I know. It is an even tougher question to answer honestly. But now might be the perfect time.

In October 2015 I attended an Alpha retreat. At the retreat they offered prayer groups that we could visit if we wished to be prayed over for various reasons. At the group I chose to approach, there were three woman offering prayers. I asked them to pray for guidance and wisdom to help me in making decisions in personal and family related matters. In my heart, I was seeking help with my man from Missouri. I was asking for prayers to know if I should be continuing this relationship or not. After the ladies prayed for me, one lady took my hands in hers and told me she felt compelled to tell me she was being drawn to tell me that she was getting a strong image of a key and a crown. She asked me if I knew what that meant? To me, in my current state of mind, I thought it must mean that the key was my son because he is the most important thing to me in my life. And I thought the crown stood for something like royalty, as in: the man in my life should treat me like a queen or he shouldn't be in my life. I thought the images she was telling me about made perfect sense!

Is it possible that those images could mean something else?

The date stamp in my journal now is November 18, 2015. I have enlisted the help of a Catholic counselor. With her help and the weekly Alpha group, I have been able to determine that I definitely have some "non-negotiables" for my relationship with the man from Missouri—or any man that I want to be with in the future. I believe the reason I have been doubting if I was doing the right thing with him was not all because of my past, but also because I was not being true to what was important to me. In my marriage, we did not put God first. We did not place Him at the center of all our decisions. If my new relationship (or any relationship, for that matter) had a chance for survival, I needed it to be focused in the right direction.

I realized that the deal-breaker for the man that would be in my life and my son's life would be this: He must be willing and able to have God be a part of our relationship and our family. I want to go to church as a family and raise my son in the church with a strong faith base. After realizing this truth, I got up the courage to bring up this topic with my boyfriend.

After at least three attempts at this conversation, he flat out said no. He would not go to church with us. I told him then that he was choosing to break up with me because he was not willing to do the one thing that was the most important thing to me. He said, "I'm not saying that, you are."

It was clear to me that he was trying to turn this around on me and make it my issue. When I discussed this conversation with my Catholic counselor, she agreed with me, saying that he was trying to turn it around and make me the "bad guy." She corrected this thought by telling me what he was really telling me was that he does not care what is important to me. To emphasize this point even further, she explained that she believed his statements should show me that he doesn't love me enough to put my needs/wants or what is good for my son ahead of his own opinions or feelings. Then she told me that I deserve that! She said I deserve to be loved by someone that is willing to put me and my wants or needs ahead of his own. Certainly, my son deserves to have a father in his life that recognizes the importance of God and regular attendance and exposure to faith in his life above sleeping in on Sundays or playing soccer. The absolute truth that I was hearing from my therapist was this: I deserve someone who values my feelings!

In the beginning of December 2015, I finally mustered up the courage to take myself to a reconciliation service. I must admit, it felt so good to get on the right side of God! To confess (what God already knew) that I had been living in sin with a man that was not my husband, even though I loved him, was liberating. I was still held bound by my marriage vows within the eyes of the church, although my husband had left me. It was up to me to take responsibility to confess my sins and ask for forgiveness and to avoid the near occasion of sin to come. It felt even better to be able to go to communion again! To "allow Jesus to enter under my roof" was humbling and I felt strengthened by his presence in my life more closely. No small feat in itself... It felt like I was running to Jesus. Literally running to him! So glad to be back in his presence that I was running to greet him!

It is amazing to me when I truly think about it, the number of miracles that I have been exposed to over the short course of time that I have been paying attention to in these moments since my husband came home and told me he was unhappy in our marriage. On December 8, 2015 I was blessed with yet another miracle to happen to me. December 8, 2015 was the day I attended mass for the Feast for the Immaculate Conception of Mary. At each mass I attend, I always try to devote the mass to someone in my life or someone I know may need a little extra prayer. Last year at this mass, I offered this Feast day mass to my (ex) husband's mom and my own mom.

On this day, I considered offering it for my ex-husband because I felt he needed all the extra prayers I, or anyone, could offer him. As I knelt in my pew, staring up at a beautiful statue of the virgin Mary, I asked her for whom to offer up this mass. All at once I felt this intense, almost overwhelming interior voice telling me to dedicate the mass to Ava—HER-- my ex-husband's new wife. She is the woman I blame for my whole life crashing. As soon as that thought entered, I thought right away, "NO! I don't want to!"

Almost immediately after that thought, a conflicting thought entered my mind, as if I were having a conversation with the Blessed Mother. At first, my thoughts were like, *"Should I be arguing with the Blessed Mother? I don't think I should tell her no."* But I did not want to give my husband's partner in adultery anything else. She had already won, in my mind. She had taken my husband: the one thing that I loved so much in this world besides my parents and siblings. The more I thought though, the more Mary's compassionate voice resonated within my heart. "Okay," I said to Mary. "You've done so much for me. Okay. This mass is for you. If you want this; if you want me to offer this mass for Ava, then okay. I will do this because you ask me to."

I then remembered that Pope Francis had declared this new liturgical year the year of MERCY. And this new year was starting today, December eighth. So, for the first time, I sincerely-- with all my heart-- with tears leaking out of my eyes-- I offered that mass, and all my prayers within it for HER. And I was able to feel that those tears were tears of relief. And they were tears of release. And they were tears of faith. Because in the moments of that mass, Our Mother Mary helped me realize that my ex-husband was now Ava's burden to bear, not mine. With the reluctant offering of that mass that I willingly gave, my heart lifted, and I was able to physically feel the release of the tight hold that I still had, even 18 months after my divorce. Mary was able to drag my pain away from me a little bit more, and I felt lighter as I walked out of the church that starry night in December. By allowing myself to offer a mass for the woman that helped my husband to end our marriage, I was truly starting down the road to forgiveness. Most of all, I was being given the miracle of MERCY for myself, even as I thought I was giving it to others.

Sometime soon after that, I decide to take another chance on applying for an annulment. I met with Father Michael to discuss my situation, my options, and any possibilities that may be available to me. It was not that I was ready to get married again, I just wanted the opportunity, should it present itself. I also wanted some assurance from God that I was going to be okay, that I could get past this failed marriage, that maybe it wasn't my fault, or if it was my fault I could get past it with his help and figure out how to do better if given another chance. Or that maybe it was not anyone's fault and that maybe the sacrament never took place for us during our wedding ceremony like I thought it did. Ultimately, I do not believe that it is my calling to be alone in this world and I needed the annulment process to help heal me to be able to truly love again. Because I do not think it is about how much we are able to love others, but maybe it is about the amount that we allow ourselves to be loved. And I really needed to allow myself to be loved as much as possible. I needed to allow myself to open to the power of God's love so that I could then open to the love of another man. Truly.

23

The Key and the Crown

In January 2016, my church sponsored a women's retreat in which they promise an all-day spiritual renewal complete with prayer, camaraderie, motivational speakers, wine, and chocolate! I signed up. I had never been to a women's retreat before, so why not? I felt as if it's been on my heart to write this story, maybe share it with others that may need to hear it for whatever reason, and I had the thought that attending this retreat would steer me in the right direction. Little did I know how inspired my thinking really was!

A woman named Lisa was the main speaker for the conference. Our pastor had heard her speak at another conference and insisted that our parish bring her out to inspire our retreat. How right he was! Lisa spoke to us about how relational women are. How we were made to relate... not only to each other as women, but to others and humanity as a whole. Through her talks, she made such valid points about God using the women in the church to "Heal My Body." As if Christ himself had inspired her to start a movement to inspire other women to share their stories to help heal the church. So that is what she has done.

Being so touched and moved by her talks, I mustered up the courage to go and talk to her during one of the breaks. I asked her how she got started talking to large groups of people. She shared with me some of her background story, I purchased her book, and she autographed it for me. Before I walked away, she told me about a pilgrimage to Italy she and some other women were organizing for that summer. She said if there was any way I could make it work to go on it with them it would be worth the money and the experience and I should really try to go.

I took the pamphlet and thanked her. After looking at the price, I thought there was no way I could spend that much. Even though it was reasonably priced, especially for the length of time and the first-class accommodations, I had never spent that much money on a trip of any kind before.

I kept fingering and glancing at the pilgrimage brochure throughout the rest of the retreat, however. For the following days to come, I kept thinking about it and even mentioned it to some teachers at my school. I could not get it out of my head for some reason... I started mentally going through my finances and adding up the costs to determine if there were ways that I could make it more of a possibility. I even mentioned it to my mom, who like me, considered herself a frugal spender, if not even a bargain shopper. I even said out loud that I could pawn or cash-in my wedding rings-- goodness knows they weren't being used anymore!

Days, maybe weeks passed while I continued to let this thought of a pilgrimage to Italy swirl around in my brain. One morning I woke up with a jolt! I had the clear answer given to me in my dreams. I called my mom right away. "Mom," I said. "I'm going to Italy!" Of course, she wondered how I had made this decision and what funds I had been able to earmark in order to comfortably get myself there. "The key and the crown!" I said, barely able to spit it out without jumping through the phone in my excitement. "The Vatican City flag has a key and a crown on it! I am going to Italy!" Without any hesitation, she simply said, "I'll go with you."

Dear reader, do you remember when I was at Alpha prayer session and the women prayed over me and one of the women referenced a key and a crown? If you recall, I thought it had something to do with my son and being treated right in a relationship? The night/early dawn before I called my mom to announce my decision to go to Italy on pilgrimage, the image of the Vatican City flag was all that I could see. To me, it was clearly a sign that this was the moment for me to grasp the meaning behind the message that woman had given me months before. I was not going to walk away from this opportunity. I believe that God was clearly speaking to me here. All I had to do was listen!

On June 19, 2016 on a tour bus full of 30-some women that are strangers to me, we begin this pilgrimage to Italy not realizing that this bus full of strangers will soon become more like a tight-knit family that any of us ever expect. "Look for frozen moments," Diana tells us coining a phrase from her godmother. She explains that these are moments when memories lock in your mind to help you recall a place and time. It was 8:30 on the first full morning of our tour and we were on our way to the Monastery of San Benedetto (Saint Benedict). Lisa Cristwell was also on the bus with us and together with Diana Paese, they remind us to also see the face of God in our journey here in Italy. They advise us to see Him in the nature and the sunset, and the music, the prayer, and the voices of the Saints we visit. I also pray to get closer to God, not just to see Him, but to get closer to Him.

St. Benedict performed many miracles during his life. Today they use his medals during exorcisms because he had great power in struggles against Satan. Once, 20 men were trying to move a rock, actually a huge boulder. Benedict saw that the devil was standing atop of it. He blessed the rock, then the devil was gone, and the rock could be moved. We need to remember to ask Saint Benedict for prayers when we are struggling against evil in this world. He will surely come to our aid!

The next day on our pilgrimage was even better. We toured St. Clare's Basilica in Assisi. She is the saint from which Mother Angelica's order is started. I gave thanks to her and offered today's pilgrimage to Mother Angelica. We also toured the Basilica of Saint Francis of Assisi. This basilica has a Holy Door, which means during this, the Jubilee Year of Mercy, whoever walks through a Holy Door, then receives reconciliation and attends mass worthily will receive special indulgences towards admittance into heaven.

When you enter through the holy door of Saint Francis of Assisi's Basilica, you enter one of the most stunning churches in all of Italy. The immense space, beautiful architecture, stained glass artwork, and sculptures move you towards the crypt where Saint Francis himself is laid to rest. You descend into the earth, down the stairs to enter his earthly resting space, where he is encased in a massive, vertical, granite, tomb. People can write prayers and messages and leave them in a box for friars to prayer for them. Instead, I reach into the tomb and touch the granite tomb and whisper prayers of healing for my ex-husband and for his family. In these moments, I could literally feel a tingling moving from the granite stone up my left hand and into my arm towards my heart! It was amazing. I have never felt something like that before.

At dinner one night, I shared my miracle story with Diana Paese and some of the other women sitting near me at the dinner table. I opened up about the pain of my divorce and the heartbreaking events leading up to the destruction of our marriage. I shared with them about my head injury, and then the miraculous gift of my son and his adoption. They were just as astounded as I am every time I think about how gracious and wonderful God has been to me! Diana invited me to be on her radio show the next day. I agreed, thinking we would be taping the episode and she could edit it for content.

The morning of the taping of the broadcast of my story began with an early morning mass at St. Clare's. Due to the reconstruction of the larger section of the church, the mass was held in the original, smaller section and conducted in Italian. About a third of the way through the service, my chest began tightening and it became a bit of a struggle to breathe freely. I started to sweat a little and get more clammy feeling. I felt as if a great oppression were weighing on my chest and my lungs could not expand. In fact, it felt like a darkness was trying to battle with me. Back in 2013, when I hit my head and I was struggling to sit up after my concussion and my head was so heavy, was a remarkably similar feeling to this day. Except this day, I was sitting in the middle of an ancient, blessed church feeling a malevolent force trying to battle with me. Thoughts were swirling in my mind as if I had to run out of the church, or that I might get sick or pass out. I had to force myself to breathe. I purposely had to envision my guardian angel with me. I uttered the prayer to Saint Michael the Archangel for protection. I was getting the distinct impression that forces were trying to make me feel like I could not fulfill my mission to share my story this day.

When I showed up at the makeshift studio, Lisa Cristwell was there as well as Lois Tripp, also a part of this wonderful pilgrimage I had been blessed to be a part of. Both women were no strangers to being guests on Catholic radio shows before. Lois had even starred in her own tv show on the network! Lisa met me in the hall, asking me if I was ready to talk on the radio. "Sure," I said. "Diana's just taping me, so she can edit any mistakes I make." Lisa laughed, then told me that no, we were doing a live broadcast. My face must have turned ashen with fear because Lisa grabbed my hand and told me not to worry, that I would be fine. She and Lois would be with me if I needed them.

I offered a quick Hail Mary as we walked into the studio/storage room where we would be broadcasting and asked the Holy Spirit to guide my words. I wanted His truth to be told so that anyone that could benefit from my experiences to be able to hear what they needed to hear in the coming moments. I was remembering so many moments of my own when I would watch EWTN and listen to Catholic Radio on my way to work and feel peace and comfort when nothing else in this world seemed to be able to help me. I prayed that my words were able to help someone else in need on this day.

The next 20-30 minutes are pretty much a blur as I spoke from my heart. I sometimes go back to the tape to listen to my story and I laugh because Diana says at one point after my story is told that was the first time she'd ever seen Lois Tripp speechless for that long of a period of time. I know there were tears in these wonderful women's eyes, as there were tears in my eyes as well. But as my pastor once said: Tears are okay because tears are just liquid love.

On June 22, 2016 we were on our way to Cascia, Italy. We were going to visit the Basilica of Saint Rita. This basilica contained another holy door to help celebrate the Jubilee Year of Mercy. During this pilgrimage, we would enter through seven holy doors. What an amazing blessing! During this trip to Cascia, I would again experience another interesting and heart-touching moment: a frozen moment, to borrow Diana Paese's words.

"By their fruits you will know them…" I wrote these words from Matthew 7:16 in my journal after our tour of Cascia. There were several memorable moments during this day. The beautiful story of Saint Rita is the first: She was married into a difficult situation at a young age and spent countless years being patient and kind to her cruel and abusive husband. She eventually won him over through her acts of kindness and changed his spirit.

As was common in her day, there was strife between her husband's family and another. When her husband was killed, her sons vowed vengeance. Saint Rita prayed that the evil welling up in her sons' hearts would be prevented or else they be allowed to die before committing any evil acts. God granted her prayers; her sons fell sick and died within a year, within the state of grace, before they acted upon their anger.

All alone in the world, Rita desired to enter the convent. To keep peace among the feuding families, she was denied entrance. Eventually, however, she was granted admittance and became known as a holy and prayerful nun despite being given the lowliest and often demeaning tasks to perform. For example, the head mistress would send Rita out to the courtyard daily to water a dead and wasting vine. Through Rita's care and obedience, and Divine intervention, this dead vine began to thrive and grow. Today, in the courtyard at St. Rita's Basilica the vine has become a large tree, extending up the side of the monastery and arching over the courtyard providing magnificent shade for visitors. It is an amazing and glorious sight!

There, in a vestibule of the basilica, is a wonderful and beautiful painting of what Saint Rita must have looked like in life. She was an exceptionally beautiful woman. One day, while praying before a crucifix, she received a visible wound on her forehead. This was said to be like a thorn, much like that from the crown of thorns from Christ's own head during his crucifixion. Despite her earthly beauty, Rita had to go through may years covering up these stigmata on her forehead, as it was said to be a ghastly wound. She suffered through this mystical experience and enjoyed many others during her life at the convent. Though she suffered many disappointments and sorrows, she closely united her life with Jesus. She is now the Patron Saint of Impossible Causes. Pray to her, ask her for intercession and prayers if you should struggle with anything in this world from infertility, abuse, loneliness, marriage difficulties, parenthood, widowhood, sickness, bodily ills, or wounds.

To this day, the body of Saint Rita is incorrupt. Her body is venerated at the basilica named for her in Cascia, Italy as her body has not decomposed. While we were there, we purchased roses from the grounds, and I prayed in the church before the body of Saint Rita. The time was between 11:00 and 11:30 a.m. For some reason, maybe it was because she is the patron saint of impossible causes, specifically in my mind infertility, that I began to pray for my sister and her husband. I knew they were trying to start a family. I also knew the heartbreak of my own heart, having suffered through miscarriages and a failed adoption. I prayed that her new family would be blessed with health and that she knows the amazing blessing of motherhood someday.

While praying I received an excruciating, sharp pain in my left side where my ovary is located. I doubled over, wondering what in the world was this? After a few moments, the pain subsided, I continued my prayers for my sister and eventually went on about my day.

Returning to the hotel early that evening, I received a phone call from my sister's husband. Why was he calling? What had happened? He quickly told me my sister was in the emergency room, across the ocean, back home in Illinois. My heart quickened and my breathing slowed… "What's wrong," I asked him.

He quickly explained, his voice catching with his own fear and anxiety very present. "She's going into surgery. She has an ectopic pregnancy and her fallopian tube ruptured."

I asked him quietly if she were there, could I talk to her? He passed her the phone and she got on the line quickly. As he did so, I mouthed to my mom who was on the line.

"They have to take the baby," my sister was crying on the phone. "We didn't even know I was pregnant. I don't want the baby to die…" She was very distraught. She thought it would be her fault for killing the baby if she let the doctors do surgery on her.

"Adalie!" I said. "It's going to be okay. You need to calm down. This is a matter of life and death now. You do not have a choice, sweetie. This is not killing your baby. The doctors need to take you into surgery to save you. If you do not go in now, you could die. God will take care of you and your baby. You just ask the hospital to call the priest so the baby can be baptized. They have had to do this before, I'm sure. They will know what to do. You need to relax and let them do their jobs, okay?" After that, my mom spoke with her and her husband, assuring them both everything would be ok and that they were doing the right thing-- really the only thing they could do!

When we hung up the long-distance call, the real miracles started taking place. Diana, Lisa, and Lois were right there by our sides, asking what happened. They immediately encircled us and formed a prayer circle around us. This relational power of the women on this pilgrimage was so comforting and so very needed. These women went even further and enlisted the power of prayer with all the women in the tour group.

By the morning we were assured that everyone had prayed for our family, and specifically my sister, over the course of the night. As we began our journey on this new day, my heart felt a little lighter due to the abundance of prayers bolstering us. We had also received word from home that my sister's surgery had gone well, the lost baby had been baptized, and my dad and brother had been with my sister and her husband during this time of need. God had wrapped his loving arms around our family since we were thousands of miles and an ocean away. Our small but mighty group of women on pilgrimage were headed to the Vatican today to have mass and then on to the Basilica of St. Mary Major, the oldest church in the world that was dedicated to Mary. If I had to be away from my sister (and my mom away from her youngest daughter in her hour of need) where better could we be than in the heart of our Church?

Entering the Vatican that morning was almost surreal. It was like we were particularly important people, like celebrities but better because we were gaining access to God's palace on earth. It was as if Moses was parting the Red Sea in the year 2016 and the Red Sea was all the other people visiting the Vatican. Surely, Diana Paese, Lois Tripp, and Lisa Cristwell pulled some strings or God had special intentions for us because we were blessed with having a special mass presided over by the Cardinal down under the St. Peter's monument, atop the very tomb that the great saint is buried! I was completely amazed to be in the presence of such a blessed space. I felt so honored to be a part of such a wonderful audience. I prayed fervently in these moments for my sister, especially.

After mass, we were further blessed to be able to meet the Cardinal, to kiss his ring and beg of him a prayer for my sister, to which he graciously agreed. He also blessed the special articles that we had purchased throughout our journey thus far. Because of this, I have some incredibly special artifacts from this pilgrimage that I believe continue to strengthen my journey to this day. Whenever I feel a particularly stressful day ahead of me, I wear the ring from Cascia, Italy that bears the resemblance of St. Rita. Not that I think it has "special powers" or anything, but it reminds me of my trip to that wonderful place and bolsters my faith that God is with me and with him all things are possible.

Another example is the small trinket I have hanging by my laundry room door, next to the garage exit. It is my St. Benedict plaque that was blessed. I trust that when I pray for protection prayers, St. Benedict will come to my aid and my home will be guarded. For me, it is little things like this that help me stay strong in this daily battle with the enemy. Though my marriage is over, and the divorce is final, the battle is far from over. I am determined to stay strong and wait for God's glory to continue to rain down on this world through me. Whatever my small part is to play, I will do my best.

24

⁂

Love What Loves You Back

Coming home from that pilgrimage, my spirit was renewed, and I knew that my mission was clear. I had to get my story out. But first, I had to make my homelife right. If I were not living my best life how could I help other people? What is easy is not always what is best. I had to brace myself for a tough conversation with my then boyfriend: the man from Missouri.

That was one of the hardest things I have ever put myself through. Breaking up with someone, I think, may just be harder than being broken up with. Being the victim is easier than taking the burden of hurting someone else. I hated seeing him broken, hurting, and with tears in his eyes. The worst part was that I still had feelings for him! I thought I could have married that man, if only he would have agreed to my deal breaker: putting God first. Why was that asking so much for him? But I have prayed about it and the answer is clear. There is no marriage to this man in my future, so I must move on and see what is in God's perfect plan for me and for my son. God can move mountains if he chooses. He could surely move this man's heart too if it was His will. My job is to be patient and wait. To trust in Jesus and keep praying.

And so, I wait. Some days the waiting seems like an eternity of nothingness. Sometimes it feels like I am walking beside Jesus carrying my own excruciatingly heavy cross right along with him. I know this image may sound self-centered, as he is always the one carrying the cross for all of us, but I'm only human and I DO feel like being a single mother is a cross sometimes, even though I gladly accepted it and would do it all over again. Again, and again, and again! The guilt I feel for not being enough for my son is sometimes overwhelming. I want him to have a good dad. A really good, loving dad that is there for him 24/7. My son is so wonderful, he deserves the best that this world has to offer, and I want to give that to him. And, to be honest, there are times when I am lonely and want love and someone to love. I do wonder when will it be my time for that wonderful feeling of compassion and companionship again? It reminds me of the verse from the Isaiah 21:11, "Watchman, how much longer the night?"

During the night, I dreamt that my true husband was back. All his mental issues were gone, the man that I had married was back in full. I dreamed that we were back together, and we were planning our reconciliation wedding. This time around, he was engaged in the process: picking out the colors of the wedding, helping me go to the flower shop, placing candles on the tables at the reception house. In my dream he was so loving and affectionate, it was exactly like it used to be, only more intense. In my dream I could feel how much we both loved each other, and we were saying it to each other all day, it was so romantic. The feeling of working together to build the life together was abundant in the dream. I awoke feeling happy and hopeful... reading this years later I realize at that time I was nowhere near ready for my heart to move on, much less my annulment to be approved despite my best intentions. Further proof that God knows what he is doing. I am glad I wrote that dream down. Not so I could relive my foolishness, but so that I could see the reality in the wisdom of God's timing. As a simple human, I want to just move on, hurry up, forget. But God knows I need to heal. I may be simple, but my heart is complex. I love deeply and God knows the truth of my heart. I trust God knows how best to heal it.

One night in November 2016 I was attending a school board meeting and received one of the most unexpected, yet inspirational messages. It was from Coach Lucas, the varsity boys' basketball coach at Central High School. He was speaking about his recent success with the basketball team and he said, "Love the things that love you back." Those simple words grabbed my attention and made me do a double take towards the coach. "Love the things that love you back," he repeated. It made me begin to think deeply about my current situation, my job, my desire to write, my hope to share this story with others, and what in general did I love in life.

"Love the things that love you back" have become a sort of mantra in my mind over the last few years for me. When I get stressed or over worked, or start to worry about particulars I ask myself, *"Do you love this? Is it giving you joy?"* If my answer is no, I force myself to stop stressing about it, because I know that "this too shall pass." For it says in Corinthians 4:17-18, "For our light and momentary troubles are achieving for us eternal glory that far outweighs them all. So, we fix our eyes not on what is seen, but on what is unseen, since what is seen is temporary, but what is unseen is eternal."

On May 23, 2018 I walk out to my mailbox and see there is a letter inside from the Diocesan Office of the Tribunal. With shaking hands, I carefully open the letter, as if disrespecting the envelope itself would change the fate of the contents inside. The decision inside this letter could be my ticket to a life of freedom or my sentence to a life behind matrimonial prison bars… What did God have in store for my life? Would my prayers be answered? In Ephesians 5:14 I find, "This is why it is said: "Wake up, sleeper, rise from the dead, and Christ will shine on you."

What, truly, was my greatest hope here? For years I did not really, genuinely want this annulment… Now, I believed I did. Five years had passed since the state of Illinois had granted us a divorce, even against my wishes. But today, I was over the past. Someone once told me people can change, but they cannot change back. I was ready for the rest of my healing to begin. The granting of this annulment would be the final phase of my healing I believed. It would allow me to profoundly move on, start over, and let go let God.

I reached into the envelope and pulled out a single sheet of paper. I wanted to read each word slowly, in order to absorb the full weight of the decision. But I could not wait; my patience, or lack thereof, forced my eyes to scan the letter until I found the decision statement I was searching for: APPROVED. Approved! My annulment had been approved!! My marriage was finally decreed null. I expected tears to come, but they did not. My hands stopped shaking and I reread the entire contents of the letter. My application for annulment had been approved, the official stamp from the tribunal had been applied to the paperwork. My marriage, almost five years to the day of the civil divorce, had finally been decreed null by the Catholic Church. I was free to marry again. In fact, the very definition of the word null was as if it had never taken place, as to not exist. By the power of the Holy Spirit I was granted the gift of having never been married.

Later that day, when I really had time to sit and try to absorb the enormity of the decision of the tribunal, I remembered the words of my ex-husband when the first application for annulment was denied. He told me, "Just try again, CeCe. That's your thing." At the time I wasn't sure if he meant the Catholic Church was my thing, or not giving up was my thing. The truth is, they are both "my thing!" This is when the tears finally did start to flow. Not as hot and fast as they once did, but more slowly and finally. When they came on this day, it was like a cleansing Spring rain, refreshing and renewing, both bittersweet and desired in its coolness. I had thought it before, right after the divorce, as I sat alone in a dimly lit bar, but the same words came back to me now, but with a lighter, more hopeful spirit: IT IS FINISHED.

It is now July 2018. I write the following entry in my journal: *As a forty-something-year-old, divorced (annulled), single mother who is waiting on her chance at happiness again, I often ponder and wonder if others do too: What am I waiting for? Why don't I hurry up and scoop up a man and make a new life for myself and young son?*

One night it suddenly came upon me like a bolt of lightning. I was waiting for my fairy tale moment. I expected my Prince Charming to come find me. Somehow, someway, I knew I deserved and expected true happiness to make its way to me. I did not want to settle! I wanted love, and passion, and excitement! I wanted my stomach to do flip-flops and for my heart to race when I gazed upon him... whoever him is...

And so, I wait. And trust that God knows what is in my heart. And, I ask God for another small favor: If HE could bless me... and my son with this kind of earthly love...

As I wait, I reflect on my lessons and I remind myself that God's plans are better than my plans. I remember that things happen in God's time, not ours. And with God's grace I have been blessed with patience and calm in this time.

Jeremiah 29:11, "For I know the plans I have for you," declares the Lord, "plans to prosper you and not to harm you, plans to give you hope and a future."

CPSIA information can be obtained
at www.ICGtesting.com
Printed in the USA
LVHW111417160421
684723LV00034B/789